Golden Snapshots
Real Stories by Real People

Complied by

Askew, D'Angelo and Greene

THE HUMANITIES COMMITTEE OF THE WAYNE
COUNTY COUNCIL FOR THE ARTS, HISTORY AND
HUMANITIES

authorHOUSE®

AuthorHouse™
1663 Liberty Drive, Suite 200
Bloomington, IN 47403
www.authorhouse.com
Phone: 1-800-839-8640

First published by AuthorHouse 8/27/2008

ISBN: 978-1-4343-8741-7 (sc)
ISBN: 978-1-4343-8983-1 (hc)

Printed in the United States of America
Bloomington, Indiana

This book is printed on acid-free paper.

Acknowledgments

This book was made possible through a grant made by Cadillac Asphalt LLC and the encouragement of the Wayne County Council for the Arts, History and Humanities. Cover art was provided by Chesley Odom of Chesley Odom Design.

Dedication

We dedicate this book to the millions who have pleasant memories of their leisure time activities in the Detroit Metropolitan Area a half century ago and to this day. We would especially honor those many unnamed persons who made our pleasures possible, the white-gloved ladies who ran the elevators, the itchy-wool suited ushers at the theaters and the waiters and cooks at the restaurants we enjoyed. As Bob Hope so often sang, "Thanks for the memories."

Contents

Introduction

"Golden Snapshots" is intended to gather an album of memories of the late 1950s in the Detroit Metropolitan Area. In an attempt to maintain fidelity with those interviewed, the editors have tried to preserve their words and phrases. The glimpses into the recreational pastimes and social activities were to be focused on that period. The essayists and persons interviewed were given the freedom to express themselves as they wished. The result contains the varied and individual commentaries of the authors. The collection of materials is, as much of the Detroit area is, color-blind. Ethnic and racial identities are undefined as you turn the pages of this album. Relaxation in the Detroit area was both diverse and integrated at the same time. The project of compiling the source material, interviewing, preparing the articles, and work on revisions was the result of the efforts of the editors to bring an album of word pictures with as much authenticity as possible. The material in this volume was collected by the Humanities Committee of the Wayne County Council for the Arts, History and Humanities.

Foreword

    1957 to 2007…A Golden Anniversary often encourages reminiscences and so it is with this book. But, this is not a story of overcoming hardship and struggling for achievement. This is a glimpse into the happier side of life. "I'm so glad that you asked me to write this, it caused me to bring back so many happy memories," wrote one contributor. The goal of this book was to do just that, to bring back the happy memories. The purpose was to advance the understanding of what people were doing in their leisure time a half-century ago. While many of the places and activities have disappeared or been severely altered, there is a permanency of satisfaction in the memories.

Belle Isle
By Diana A. Hage

As long as I can remember Belle Isle was always a paradise island to this gal from the city of Detroit. Not too many of us had the luxury of air-conditioning back then so when the weather was unbearably hot we would pack a picnic lunch and head for Belle Isle. My parents chose an area near the Coast Guard Armory where they met their ethnic friends. The mothers laid out the picnic food and after we ate a hearty meal, our poor mothers cleared the table while the men retreated to play cards. Then when the women finally finished their clean-up work they would relax by the shore of the Detroit River in their lawn chairs and soak their feet in the water. The children would be busy playing and climbing trees but never too busy to observe the large freighters passing by. Of course our mothers would be so busy chatting they would not notice that when the freighters passed the shoreline receded only to rebound a few moments later and get them all soaked. They would jump up yelling and we would be hiding and laughing.

Another hilarious moment for the kids that would send us into barrels of laughter was in the event of a sudden downpour of rain our mothers would gather up the picnic baskets while looking up at the sky and yell "shitty, shitty". Now, most non-Lebanese did not know that the Arabic word for rain is "shitty" so they would be wondering why profanity would be spewing out of the mouths of these otherwise respectable women. Yes, I have many wonderful memories of Belle Isle and now I take my grandchildren there to experience the thrill of the many attractions that now are available to them while I sit and reminisce about my own childhood.

Let's Do Lunch
By Gerry Tamm

One beautiful fall day in 1957, I took my place in line at the entrance to Hudson's twelfth floor dining room. Not the long line on the left, but the shorter line on the right where singles who wished to share a table waited their turn to be seated. Over the years I had shared lunch with many interesting strangers. I never had an unpleasant experience.

That day was a treat for myself, a day free from the care of my first baby who was at home with his grandmother. How better to spend it than at Hudson's much like teenagers these days who hang out at the mall. The only decision I had to make at that moment was whether to have the legendary Maurice salad with its unique dressing or the equally legendary chicken pot pie loaded with white meat chicken and rich yellow gravy, unlike the more common conglomeration of vegetables laced with chicken at other places. How many times had I made that choice!

I had parked my brand new turquoise Rambler station wagon in the structure on Broadway across from Broadway Market and Midwest Woolen–where I often shopped for fabric–walked the block to Hudson's back door and headed for the express elevator that whisked me up to the thirteenth floor without a stop. The young woman operator in her snappy uniform with the gold braid trim and shiny buttons and her white gloves stopped the car smoothly, precisely even with the opening, slid the heavy brass gate open and the passengers emerged.

As I waited in line I thought of the many lunches I had eaten here and in the other Hudson restaurants since my mother first brought me here as a child. We would stash our coats in a locker on the fourth floor, have our shoes shined across the hall, and then get down to our shopping. Most of our clothes and household goods came from Hudson's, much of it delivered to our door by the green delivery truck and the friendly driver.

As teens my best girl friend and I would dress up in our hats and gloves–not like the jeans, tee shirts, and flip-flops girls wear these days–and take the bus downtown to spend the day. We would have lunch in the less formal mezzanine restaurant, nut bread– perhaps date nut or banana nut–supreme, that delicious concoction of cream cheese and strawberry jam, a standard on the menu.

In my working years I would walk to Hudson's from the Penobscot building on my lunch hour and head for the soda fountain, the counter behind the mezzanine restaurant, Hudson's version of fast food. I would choose the diner who looked closest to being finished, and take my place behind him or her with the others waiting for a stool. One of my favorite lunches was egg salad on dark rye bread with a lemon milk shake. There should have been an entertainment charge for the show put on by the group of waiters who had worked there for years. They wrote up their orders on a pantograph that somehow transmitted them to the kitchen where they were filled, then delivered on a conveyor belt to each section. The waiters never had to leave their stations. They had only to tend their customers, supply their utensils and beverages, and clear their places. The plates arrived at each station with colored plastic covers that were stopped by a system of colored lights that allowed some colors to pass and others to stop the belt. Watching the waiters was like watching a carefully choreographed dance as they twirled from customers, to the covered plates, to glasses and cups, sodas, coffee, and of course ice cream.

The line at the dining room moved quickly. I looked forward to a leisurely lunch away from the bustle and clatter of the mezzanine. Soon the hostess ushered my lunch partner and me into the dining room where quiet conversation was accompanied by the gentle clink of china and silverware muffled by carpeting and linen table cloths. We both turned our attention to the menu. I toyed with the idea of ordering a shrimp salad sandwich on toasted cheese bread, another of my favorites. But of course I succumbed. It was so long since I had been here. It had to be Maurice salad and that crusty hard roll with cold butter. I tucked my linen napkin in my lap, sipped ice water from the stemmed goblet, and chatted with my new friend as we waited for our lunch.

"Woodward Avenue Cruises AND The Burlesque Theatre... all in ONE DAY!"

By Robert Paul Szekely

I wasn't going to let anything stand in the way of me becoming an architect...not even the fact I had to go on a 'Woodward Avenue Cruise' three times a week. The Burlesque portions of these 'Cruises' were a bonus and slightly easier to abide! Let me elaborate:

I boarded the Woodward Avenue streetcar in front of the Ernst Kern (not Ernest) Department Store a little after 5:30 in the evening. Traffic was at its peak this time of day during the mid-fifties in downtown Detroit. Most of the people were heading for home, but there were a lot of folks getting off of buses to do some last-minute shopping at Hudson's, Crowley Milner's, or even Neisner's, the 'five-and-dime' store across the street. I didn't like riding these buses to my destination because they were always pulling in and out of traffic, swerving to the curb to pick up people or dropping them off. I discovered the streetcar would save me quite a few valuable minutes. Thus began my string of Woodward Avenue Cruises!

Most of the time during my 'Cruise', because of the evening crowds, I had to stand while the streetcar swayed from left to right and back again, as it made its way north on Woodward. The quick jerky stops and starts were another thing you had to get used to, as you hung on to one of the dozens of dangling black straps swaying from the ceiling of the clanging streetcar. You learned very quickly, sometimes the hard way, how to stand, shift your weight, and still be able to read the Detroit Times newspaper. Wednesday night was the only time I could get to my destination in 15 minutes because of the lighter traffic once we passed beautiful West Grand Blvd.

At this time in my life, I was working for a major Department Store in the middle of the thriving metropolis of Detroit, Michigan. I worked full-time while going to night school every Monday, Wednesday and Friday evenings. I followed this schedule for almost two years. I eventually transferred my classes and my major to Wayne State University so I could be closer to my new position in another retailing firm.

During these 'Woodward Avenue Cruises', I passed the elite J.L. Hudson Downtown Store, Kern's, and Wright Kay Jewelers. Across the street were women's shops such as B. Seigel's, Lerner's, Lane Bryant, Casual Corner, The Limited, Maryann's and Alberts. On the west side of Woodward were men's shops like Hughes and Hatcher, and Capper and Capper.

I rode the Lincoln Park bus to work in the wee hours of the morning. My wife's office hours were much later than mine. She drove our 1955 Chevy to work. At that time, she was working for an insurance company near the beautiful Grand Circus Park in the heart of downtown Detroit. She had the distinction of being able to park our one and only car in her company's lot underneath the Park. That was cool, in more ways than one!

On the northwest corner of the Park, we passed Victor Lim's eatery, and the ever-popular Brass Rail—a favorite watering hole for many of the Michigan Mutual Executives. A couple of blocks further north, we rode past the Fox Theatre and headed toward Highland Park with bells clanging. It was at the Fox where we met Caesar Romero, a handsome Hollywood leading man, who appeared on stage for a political fund-raiser convention. I got his autograph for my Aunt Helen. She was thrilled!

On the left, we passed Winkelmans' Warehouse and their Main Office. After a couple of more blocks, we approached an old used book store in a dilapidated building on the next corner.

I recall purchasing a beautiful copy of 'Proctor's Poems', an 1888 edition for only thirty cents.

One of the best buys of the Century! It was signed "To Fanny from Elizabeth Elmundorf, Christmas, 1888".

My Cruise continued further north. We saw the giant Demery's Department Store, tall and stately in the distance, a pretty good rival of Hudson's in those days. The Demery's marquee was always lit up and decorated with tons of seasonal décor that was visible from at least two blocks away.

Traffic lightened up considerably once we were north of Chicago Blvd. As the streetcar approached the city of Highland Park, I fought my way through the passengers, shoving my briefcase ahead of me, and got ready to pull the cord hanging over the windows. The conductor didn't mind if you exited at the front bi-fold doors, or the ones near the middle of the car.

We continued past at least two Winkelmans' women's stores by the time the streetcar got to the General Motors Building near West Grand Blvd. You could see the Fisher Building a block or so west of Woodward. Men's clothing stores like Harper's competed with other shops across the street from the Fisher Building. A few minutes later, the streetcar approached Davidson. The streetcar stopped at my destination…the Lawrence Institute of Technology. Cruises anyone? I have had hundreds of them!

Where do those rowdy Burlesque Houses come in that they talked about in those good old days? Read on.

A few hours later, after classes were over for the evening, I walked to the streetcar stop and took the car back toward downtown Detroit. I got off the yellow- painted structure in front of the City Hall, near Fort Street at that time. From there, I had to walk two blocks east on Monroe, towards Brush Street, to catch the Lincoln Park bus home. This was the very strange part of my trip for the day. I had to board my final bus of the day in front of the Burlesque House…the Gayety Theatre! I would stand in front of the Burlesque Theatre, waiting for the bus, looking at the very colorful posters in the large glass-framed sign-holders. That kept me busy for a few minutes. There were no coffee shops nearby for me to wait for my bus. On the cold days, I would go into the lobby of the Theatre to keep warm. I walked through the lobby, looking at the posters of the "acts" being featured during the week. I remember there were no fancy names like the stars have today in the movies and videos. I recall names like Sally or just plain Dolores from Dallas. Burlesque in this era seemed more artistic than pornographic; a far cry from today's videos, websites and movies. Ah…those wonderful mid-fifties!

The posters on the walls in the lobby and outside of the building were very conservative. The young women (sometimes they weren't very young) were photographed behind a large balloon or a basket of flowers. The pictures were not suggestive in the least. Mostly they featured women with a catchy title such as 'Chicago Bombshell!'

One cold and windy night, I was standing in the lobby trying to keep warm, waiting for the bus. It finally pulled to the curb, 15 minutes late. I hurried up the steps and boarded the bus. Sitting in the front row of seats was a young woman that looked vaguely familiar. She looked up and smiled at me. It was Janet. We had graduated a few years earlier from Lincoln Park High School. I just had a feeling she saw me come out of the theatre.

As soon as I boarded the bus, we both looked up to see about 25 people come out of the Gayety Burlesque Theatre. Janet looked at me kind of strangely.

"Did you enjoy the show?" she asked, still smiling.

"I was in the lobby to keep warm." I don't think I was very convincing. I felt this was going to be a very uncomfortable trip to Lincoln Park. I got up from my seat next to her and told Janet I was going to night school. I told her I had some homework to do. I went to the back of the bus…and I actually did start on my homework! That was the last time I saw Janet.

I fondly recall those nostalgic days in front of the Gayety Burlesque Theatre… and my wonderful Woodward Avenue Cruises in the good old Fifties! Where else can you have a Cruise and Burlesque…all in one day?

1957 – What a Wonderful Year
By Cathy Horste

1957 was a wonderful year...or at least it was as I remember it... but then I was only eleven years old!

I remember the January inauguration of Dwight Eisenhower and Richard Nixon.

My mother, who usually spoke ill of no-one, said, "I don't trust that man", referring to Nixon, and some think history proved her correct. I remember the grand opening of the Mackinaw Bridge in 1957. That's when I discovered that Michigan was bigger than its familiar mitten shape. Boy, was I surprised!

I remember G. Mennon (Soapy) Williams was governor of Michigan in 1957, (seems like he was *always* governor) and while Dad was temporarily laid off from work, he drove me to Lansing. We ran into Governor Williams in the lobby of the Capitol Building. Williams took time to shake my hand, tell me how charming I was, and suggest that I consider a career in politics. I thought that sounded like a great idea - instant celebrity!

I remember the cars of 1957, too. That was the start of the "fin" era. Fords and Chevys of '57 are the benchmark to me in classic cars today. Dad had a much older pickup truck then. The floor boards were rusted out, and we had to tie the driver's side door shut. Dad let me drive it around the yard that summer. We had a big yard, but I managed to drive that truck into our very deep ditch. I had to wait another five years before Dad let me drive again.

Mom had a great car, though. It was a bittersweet orange and white four-holer Buick Roadmaster. (Dad secretly called it a "road monster".) Mom *never* let me drive her Buick around the yard. Speaking of cars, I remember sitting on the garage floor, watching Dad cut out "W"s (I'll explain later) while he listened to the Indianapolis 500 on the radio over the Memorial Day holiday of 1957. I don't remember who won, but I do remember that Dad could always be talked into going to any race, any time, any place, including Flat Rock Speedway, and a track at the Michigan State Fair Grounds on Eight Mile Road in Detroit.

We had a television in 1957 but not everybody did. Ours was a Philco, with television, radio, and phonograph, all hidden in drawers. It had about fifty control knobs, and just like the old joke, I suspect only three of them actually worked - off/on, volume, and channel selection! The screen was approximately the size of my school lunch box! I remember Kukla, Fran and Ollie on TV, and Soupy Sales was my absolute hero! I remember watching Popeye cartoons, hosted by Poopdeck Paul on Channel 9 - the Canadian TV station. I always watched Howdy Doody, and had hopes of growing up to be Princess SummerFall WinterSpring. I remember Milky's Party Time and the silver Twin Pines insulated, home-delivery milk box on our front porch. I just knew if we got that milk delivered I, too, would be able to do magic! Now that I think about it, I was pretty gullible back in 1957. TV was the greatest back then! I remember watching Blondie, Perry Mason, Lassie, Superman, Dragnet, Jack Benny and Red Wing hockey games. (My polydactyl cat, Feetzer, always tried to catch the puck on screen.) Game shows abounded, as did cowboy shows. I remember going to Grandma's house in Dearborn for Sunday dinner, but we had to leave before Gunsmoke came on. (Grandpa was hard of hearing and no talking was allowed during Gunsmoke!)

The idea of 24-hour, around the clock TV hadn't been invented by 1957. Most stations played the "Star Spangled Banner", then went off the air after the 11PM news. Dad convinced me that law required I stand with my hand over my heart (in the living room) while the music played. (Dad was a well-known practical joker.) I remember the black and white "test patterns" that were broadcast all night, too. I remember a news report about Jimmy Hoffa's arrest by the FBI on bribery charges. (Go figure!) Union activities were always big news at our house! I remember talk of Jack Parr taking over the Tonight show, and Mom's opinion that he wouldn't last. I remember staying up late one Sunday evening to watch Elvis Pressley on the Ed Sullivan show. As I recall, censors blocked out the bottom of the screen so no one could see his hips.

'57 was a good year for radio, too. I remember "All Shook Up" by Elvis, "Bye Bye Love" by the Everly Brothers, "Singing the Blues" by Guy Mitchell, and Dad's favorite, "Round and Round" by Perry Como. Belleville had a movie theater on Main Street, so we saw lots of movies in 1957. I remember the "Bridge on the River Kwai", "Curse of Frankestein", "The Incredible Shrinking Man", and "Jailhouse Rock". Mom was dubious about letting me see that last one, so Dad had to go along with me. That was so embarrassing!

I remember the annual trip to J.L. Hudson's to buy school clothes. We parked in the Library Street parking lot and walked to the store. I didn't like the food at Hudson's because I thought it was too fancy, but I was sure impressed with those white-gloved elevator operators who called out the items available on each floor from memory. For a while, I thought that might be the career for me. I always wanted to try it but never had the opportunity. There was plenty of good food available on those trips downtown. I remember Vernors and its gnome, Sanders hot fudge, Better Made potato chips, Coney Island hot dogs (hold the mustard on mine, please), and Cherry Phosphates at a drug store there.

The Automobile Club of America (AAA) sponsored the "safety boy" program at school. Designated sixth graders were issued arm bands, and obliged to help others safely cross streets and on/off the busses. In 1957, I was honored to be a safety boy (even though I'm female). In June, AAA treated us to a trip to Briggs Stadium to see the Detroit Tigers play. That's where I got my first glimpse of future Hall-of-Famers Norm Cash and Al Kaline. I've been a Tiger fan ever since!

Led by quarterback Bobby Layne, the Detroit Lions won the National Football League Championship in 1957. I'm sure they would have won the Super Bowl that year, too, but it hadn't been invented yet. Dad took me to Willow Run Airport in Ypsilanti (Detroit Metro Airport hadn't really been invented yet, either) to meet the Lions coming home. There were no formalities back in those days - we walked right out onto the runway to wait for the plane. Once off the plane, players mingled with the crowd. One large Lion picked me up and gave me a little "toss", much to the horror of my mother. Much to the glee of my father, I was able to get autographs from Howard "Hopalong" Cassidy, John Gordy, and Bobby Layne in my little, pink, 1957 "date line" autograph book.

Edgewater Park in '57 is another wonderful memory. Dad's union rented the entire place. We could ride everything for free as often as we wanted to! It was there that I saw my first roller-coaster, and rode it while hiding under Mom's shirt! I was terrified I'd fall out, and didn't get on another coaster until Summer, 1963, when I visited Tivoli Garden in Copenhagen. My fears came true - I fell out at Tivoli, and thankfully, the only thing broken was my glasses.

Michigan history was a required class when I was in the sixth grade in 1957. My life-long love of Michigan history began there, and I was so fascinated by the tales of Pere Marquette that I named my new parakeet in his honor. My sister, Chris, was a majorette throughout high school and she was a Senior at Belleville High School when I was in sixth grade. Pere met his end in '57 when he flew under Chris's white marching boots as she practiced. I have since forgiven her, but I carried a grudge for many years. Chris married Ted in the fall of '57, in a huge ceremony at St. Anthony's Catholic Church in Belleville. I was to be the junior bride's maid, and wear a beautiful floor length gown - my first. About two weeks before the wedding, I came down with Asian Flu, ending up in Wyandotte General Hospital. I'd never heard of the flu but it sure made the rounds in 1957! It was during that hospital stay that I learned all ginger ale isn't Vernors, and I can still remember the horrible taste of the other brand. I got well in time for the wedding, but the bride and groom got the flu on their honeymoon. They will celebrate their 50th wedding anniversary this fall at their home in South Dakota.

My favorite 1957 memories are those of the Wicker family reunion. My Grandma and Grandpa Wicker were both alive, and their huge family met annually in the Lower Huron Metropark in western Wayne County. Dad made large, red, wooden "W"s, and we got up early Labor Day morning to put them out along the park drive as guides to the picnic area. Dad and I camped out in the shelter to "reserve" it, and while we waited, mom brought us bacon, eggs and hot chocolate as a treat. Mom was one of eleven Wicker children, and when all the aunts, uncles, cousins, in-laws (and out-laws) showed up, the crowd numbered well into the hundreds. Everybody brought a dish to pass. Mom always made potato salad with at least a dozen eggs in it, and she "squished" it by hand. Aunt Dee made deviled eggs by the cookie-sheet-full, and beautiful pineapple-upside-down cakes. Aunt Vi brought tubs of spaghetti, which I viewed as strange and refused to eat! Grandma brought roaster pans of baked beans made with molasses and bacon. Another Aunt always brought only a package of store-bought cookies, but there was never any shortage of delicious food to eat.

Grandma and Grandpa are long gone, and Mom is the surviving Wicker child. The family still meets every fall in the Metropark, and Dad's wooden "W"s still make their annual appearance. Traditions go on, and memories continue to be made. All in all, I'd say 1957 was a wonderful year as I remember it!

Motor City Iconoclasts
By Ken Askew

The 1957 Chevrolet has often been referred to as the icon of the time period when Woodward Avenue was the playground of auto enthusiasts of the Detroit area. That was just part of the action. As a confirmed race fan, raised to enjoy the motor competition, it was a great time to be a Motor City racing fan. I started young with my dad taking me to see the races inside the Horticultural Building at the Michigan State Fair Grounds. There the little midgets filled the building with the Castor oil rich fumes that made addicts of their admirers. Auto racing was one of the rare things that I was able to share with my Dad. By the late fifties we had become habitual observers of the racing at Motor City Speedway. The Speedway was only part of the auto racing scene around Detroit. NASCAR had had its try at the city in the early fifties, but chose not to stay on the dirt track at the Fair Grounds. On Sibley Road the National Hot Rod Association was running drag races. The Dodge Ramchargers were devoted to the old adage, "Race on Sunday and sell on Monday." At Mt. Clemens Speedway the half-mile dirt was the scene of weekly races, while South of Detroit the Flat Rock Speedway offered a quarter mile of paved surface. But, the most sensational and regular of all was the Motor City Speedway with its twice a week race schedule. On Wednesdays the motorcyclists tore around the track, balanced by an extended left foot, clad in a steel bottomed boot that kept them up. But, it was Saturday nights that my Dad and I enjoyed the most. We never sat together. He liked to watch the cars come out of the turns, with their rear wheels out to the side and their front wheels turned to counteract, the cars would shower the spectators with particles of dirt. My Dad usually ended up with a lot of dirt mixed in with his chewing gum. I preferred watching the cars entering the turn at the other end of the grandstand. There they would turn sharply to toss the car and make the rear-end swing out in the beginnings of a skid, and then they would hold that balance with the application of power; more gas to turn tighter, less to straighten. Dirt-tracking was the popular and fast way around the oval, much to the satisfaction of the fans.

It was a golden time for the automobile enthusiast, and the 1957 Chevy became the symbol of that time for thousands. It is still revered and sometimes almost worshipped.

Now, turn your attention for a moment on those who might be called iconoclasts of the motor city. These were the ones who rejected the idea that Detroit Iron should rule the road. By 1957 there were a significant number of renegades from the drag race from traffic light to traffic light that was so celebrated on Woodward Avenue. These were the non-conformists who had discovered the pleasures of automobiles that featured handling and braking.

By 1957 there were many sports car clubs that reflected the interest of drivers in such cars. The list of clubs would include: the Sports Car Club of America, The MG Car Club, the Triumph Owners Club, the Porsche Club of America, The Jaguar Owners Club, The Alfa-Romeo Owners Club, the Corvette Club of Michigan, The Ford Motorsports Club, and the Michigan Sports Car Club. All of the clubs were active and well established by 1957. 1957 became a significant year for changes in the sports car scene in Detroit.

The clubs sponsored ice runs in the Winter, with courses laid out on frozen lakes, and ice races where the sand-covered surfaces gave traction enough for wheel to wheel races. For the precision-minded there were rallies which called for precise speed-control by the driver while the navigator interpreted complex directions to keep them on course. The object was to arrive at check-points at correct pre-determined times, with a penalty for being off of the time. Many of the clubs sponsored handling contests that put an emphasis on speedy maneuvers on tight courses, usually on parking lots, these events were called Gymkhanas. Eventually a greater emphasis on speed has resulted in what is now called an Autocross.

The proliferation of clubs and events resulted in difficulties in participation due to difficulties in scheduling and variations in rules concerning the cars. Most of us who were competitors belonged to a number of clubs to keep track of events. It concerned many of us until the discussion of the problem at a social gathering at the home of Ed Houlihan. Ed later became the Starter for Mid-Ohio Race Course, but on this night he was concerned as a driver of a Morgan in local handling trials. In the midst of the conversations, Orly Ward, a local insurance broker who campaigned an Alfa-Romeo, took out his wallet and threw a bill into the middle of the group. "What we need is a Detroit Council of Sports Car clubs, and here is the money to get it started."

Not only was the Detroit Council of Sports Car Club started in 1957, but it still functions to-day as cooperatively the various clubs conduct the Championship series of handling trials called the Autocross Championship, with standardized rules for all competitors and a calendar of events.

The most serious of the sports car owners were those who were competing in road races. It was a time described by some as a period of innocent Golden times. Anyone could purchase a potential winning car at the local dealer or used car lot. Almost all of the entries at a race would be owner-driver, with only a few cars being given to another driver by owners who were anxious to see their cars perform as well as possible. We traveled to road races that were being held on the streets of towns like Watkins Glen, Elkhart Lake and Put-In-Bay. Many cars carrying the yellow tape stripes of an unofficial Detroit team were seen on the airport circuits of Illinois, Wisconsin, Ohio and Canada.

Road racing at that time required a Competition License and Detroit area drivers represented many different organizations, the Sports Car Club of America, The MG Car Club, the Canadian Auto Sports Club, The British Race Drivers Association. Once licensed a driver merely had to pick up his girl friend, a helmet and drive off to the races. At the racecourse one removed the hub caps and the loose articles in the cockpit, tightened a seat belt and went racing. For really serious races we also would take off windshields and mufflers, replacing them with the tiny Brooklands windscreens and straight pipes. The windshields did make a difference in speed, I was never sure about the mufflers, but it sounded faster and the fans loved the sounds.

Sports car road racing was primarily by three clubs. The Sports Car Club of America was the leading sponsor of road races all across the United States. The club had complex licensing methods and strong public support. The SCCA maintained extensive records of races and racers and devised a point system by which they designated national champions based upon performances in races they sponsored. Detroiters participated with cars like; Cadillac-Allard, Ferrari, BMW, Jaguar, Arnolt-Bristol, Ace, Triumph, Morgan, Abarth, Siata, Maserati, MG, Alfa-Romeo, SAAB, Porsche.

The Canadian Auto Sports Club sponsored races in Canada that were characterized by a looseness of formality and long days of practice. A Canadian week-end of racing was guaranteed to use up a set of tires. They held races based on formulas of efficiency where cars were handicapped based on previous performances. They held relay races where cars were teamed and two, three, or four cars and drivers competed.

The Michigan Sports Car Club held races in the Detroit area, at Mt.Clemens Speedway and emphasized bringing novices into racing by using dirt tracks that permitted extreme driving but at safer speeds than a paved course. They were less formal than the other clubs although they were as stringent in safety requirements and driver discipline.

All this activity caused Detroit enthusiasts to want a road-race course of their own, some place that could be used to train and develop competition drivers and be an outlet for the ambitions of local drivers.

In 1957 the popularity of racing led a group of Detroit area enthusiasts to form the Waterford Hills Sports Car Racing Club and to share the Oakland County shooting club by building a small road circuit there. As usual the issue of money became obvious. To support the efforts to provide a race course, the Michigan Sports Car Club decided to put on a race in Detroit. The Michigan State Fairgrounds had a one-half mile dirt track where late-model stock car racing was being conducted by John Marcum, founder of Midwest Association for Race Cars (MARC)

Ed Lawrence represented Michigan Sports Car Club in negotiations to secure a date and Detroit's first road race was underway. I worked with Ed's committee in the promotion of the race and watched his determination to make Detroit's Sports Car race a success. Ed loved racing although it ended his life the next year in a fiery crash of a Maserati at Sebring.

The races that were arranged for the half-mile oval included two chicanes. These obstacles required the cars to brake and maneuver, one with a left-right-left motion and the other with a right-left -right. A series of races for different classes of cars was on the program. One race was for small sedans; VW, Renault, SAAB and Skoda. Another race was for small sports cars, featuring Porsche, Alfa-Romeo and MG. Next would come the mid-size cars of Triumph, Morgan and Austin-Healy. The final race of the day would include the big performers of Corvette, Jaguar and Thunderbird.

The first practice sessions went well. Then the rain came. It only rained for about twenty minutes, but that was enough to turn the dirt track to mud. There was no way to dry the surface, but it might be possible to pack it down. An invitation was announced to ask anyone who would like to drive around the track and help pack down the dirt. The result was one of the features of the day as a Seven-up truck driver brought his loaded truck and ran some drama-filled laps on the wet dirt. Shortly the dirt was packed down and the races proceeded. I enjoyed an excellent seat in the small sports race where I watched Les Morriset win while I followed him to second place, we both had Alfas, he drove faster.

The early races were exciting enough, but the emotion and interest was intensified when the Corvettes and Thunderbirds came to the field. It needs to be noted at this point that the automobile manufacturers were officially not in racing. Corvette was taking full advantage of the improvements made to its cars by Zora Arkus-Duntov. Some privately owned and driven Corvettes were getting the benefit of having their cars at the GM Tech Center during the week while they raced them on the week-ends. Ford Thunderbirds had been suffering by comparison to the dominating Corvettes. Thunderbird drivers who had been frustrated were to be given hope. Two Thunderbirds had been built, and called the Battle-birds. The cars were all aluminum-bodied creations, shaped to look like a stock Thunderbird, built on a race car chassis, powered by a Lincoln engine coupled to a Jaguar transmission. They had completely standard chrome trim and from a distance were indistinguishable from a standard Thunderbird. One of these Battle- Birds was entered by Andy Hotton, owner of Dearborn Steel Tubing, and a Ford supplier. Making sure the car would make a good showing it was being driven by Ralph Durbin. Durbin was past National Champion in the MG class and a winner of major races with Austin-Healey and Alfa-Romeo. More than that, Ralph was a close friend and mentor to me, he let me share his Alfa- Romeo in winning at Elkhart Lake, and then sold me the car.

The outcome of the Corvette- Thunderbird race was obvious by the second lap of the 50 lap race when Durbin took the lead and drove away from all the rest to a comfortable win. As Starter in that race I was privileged to wave the checkered flag as Ralph cruised past.

The sports car races in Detroit were successful in raising the money to help Waterford Hills become one of the great training courses in the country. 1958 began the era of prize money for road racing and a close of the period of racing for only fun, pride and trophies.

Palace of Dreams
By Mono D'Angelo

My family lived in the predominantly Italian neighborhood near Mack and Van Dyke in the early 1950's. Several years later, our father moved us to the suburb of Taylor, so he would be closer to his job at the Ford Rouge Plant. I grew up in the iconic 1950's and 1960's. By 1957, I was an all-American, twelve-year-old boy.

One of the many things twelve-year-old boys loved to do was go see a movie in one of the grand, old theaters of downtown Detroit. The Michigan, United Artist and Fox attracted movie goers from all around Detroit and its suburbs. One of my most vivid 1957 memories is of just such a night in one of those magical movie palaces.

My two best friends were Lee Cagle and Frank Little. We played sandlot baseball and football together, built our tree forts in the woods near Lee's house and all went to the same school. There were not many days we didn't hang out together.

One afternoon, while looking through the Detroit News funny pages, I spotted an advertisement for a film every twelve-year old boy absolutely had to see. I tore the ad from the paper, ran out of the house and hopped on my old newspaper bicycle. I rode to Frank Little's house as fast as I could.

"FrankiEEE," I shouted in a melodic, half scream. He came out onto the small, cement porch, eating the last few bites of a fried egg sandwich and said, "What the heck are you shouting about?"

"Look at this," I yelled, waving the ad in his face. "We got to go downtown to the movies tomorrow night. It's the last night and you'll never guess what's playing."

"Let me see that, will ya. I don't have a lot of time," he said, grabbing the ad. "American Bandstand is coming on in a few minutes."

"It's The Phantom of the Rue Morgue, with Karl Malden," I blurted out, "and it's in 3-D."

"Wow! No joke? That's really cool."

"Yeah. The show starts at 7:30. If we catch the 5:00 o'clock bus, we can get there in plenty of time. I'm gonna ride over to Lee's and tell him we're going. See ya later," I shouted. I jumped back on my bike and sped away.

I came from a large family, so there was no money for luxuries like going downtown to a movie. If I wanted to go, I had to pay for it myself. I had a paper route, worked as a part time window cleaner at a nearby car wash for ten cents a car and picked up trash at the Ecorse Drive-in on weekends. I could earn enough money to pay for the bus ride, the movie and have enough left over for a late night meal at the classy Flaming Embers Restaurant.

The following evening, Frankie and I walked to Lee's house, knocked on the door and waited in the foyer until he came down from his upstairs bedroom. Lee had four older sisters, so Frankie and I didn't mind waiting around for him. After he bounced down the stairs, he looked us straight in the face and said, "You guys having a good time?" We all laughed, headed out the door and walked along the dirt path behind his house. The path led to our make shift baseball diamond in the weed choked field behind his house. The bus stop was on the corner of Mortenview and Ecorse Roads, about a good fastball away from first base.

For three pre-teen boys from the car dominated suburbs, going downtown to a movie was as close to being grown-ups as we could get. We were too young, too poor and too irresponsible to drive, but walking around Grand Circus Park after the sun went down brought us to the edge of our future. I remember how anxious those evenings made me to reach my sixteenth birthday and get my driver's license.

We all tried our best to dress older than we really were, like the teen idols of that time. Frankie and Lee wore colored shirts with the collars up, like Elvis Presley. I wore tight jeans and a white tee shirt, trying to look as much like James Dean in "Rebel

Without a Cause" as I could. I even snuck a pack of Camel cigarettes from my father's carton and rolled them up in my tee shirt sleeve. I didn't know how to really smoke, but that didn't matter to me. With more than a little dab of Brylcream in our hair to get our waterfall and ducktail hairdos just right, we were ready to go to the movies.

The five o'clock bus arrived on schedule and we climbed aboard.

"Evening boys," said Nate the driver.

"Hiya Nate," we all replied, as we deposited our fare into the coin collector.

"Where you guys going all spiffed up?"

"To the movies," I replied. "Phantom of the Rue Morgue is playing at the United Artist tonight. And it's in 3-D."

"3-D, eh? Well that should be a good one."

"It's supposed to be real scary," Frankie chimed in.

"The way you guys are all dressed up, looks more like you're going to meet some girls instead of a movie," Nate said with a chuckle.

Girls had started to become an important part of my life by then, but I recall being a little embarrassed when Nate confronted me about it. I laughed nervously and merely shrugged my shoulders as the bus headed toward Detroit.

The hour long bus ride ended at Grand Circus Park and Woodward Avenue. There were only a few passengers besides Frankie, Lee and I, and as we exited the bus, Nate said, "Remember, the last bus leaves from this stop at eleven o'clock."

"We know," we all shouted in unison.

The United Artist Theater was a short walk from the bus stop. It was located on Clifford Street, between Bagley and Adams. We walked south on Bagley and once we got to Clifford, the brilliantly illuminated marquee came into view. The glowing white glass façade was capped by a deep, red crown proudly displaying her name. On the marquee below the theater name, in bold, black letters was the reason we were there. "PHANTOM OF THE RUE MORGUE – 3D" I still recall thinking that was what great theaters must have been like in Hollywood during the movie heydays of the mid 1940's.

Our pace quickened as we neared the theater. The box office resembled an oversized bronze and glass vault. Inside, the ticket usher, dressed in a burgundy coat, black tie and small, pill box hat, spoke through a small, round hole in the glass.

"How many, please?"

"I'll take one," I said.

"That'll be seventy-five cents."

I fumbled through my pocket for three quarters and slid them through the window slot. The ticket machine whirred and moments later, my ticket appeared through a pop up dispenser in the bronze counter top. The ticket usher then handed me a pair of folded, cardboard glasses with red and green lens. "Put these on once the movie starts," he instructed.

With a ticket and 3D glasses in hand, I pulled open the heavy glass doors, gave my ticket to the usher and entered the spectacular lobby.

I'd been to a few shows near my home, but none could compare to the opulence of the United Artist. The unique round lobby was a collage of glistening, marble floors and walls, luxurious red carpet and elegant burgundy curtains hanging from all the entrance ways. Bronze posts with bright red velvet ropes were everywhere, directing patrons throughout the theater. On many walls, there were mirrors decorated with hand-crafted plaster mosaics. The lobby ceiling was at least three stories high, supported by several giant columns resembling European art deco more than downtown Detroit. On the ceilings, large, ornate bowls, gently backlit in a variety of soft colors added a sense of elegance. The glitzy refreshment counter completed the wonderful visual experience.

The aroma of hot dogs roasting on a rotating drum of shiny spikes was irresistible.

"Let's get a hot dog and a Coke," I said in a quiet voice. The grandeur of the lobby had commanded a quiet respect from my friends and me.

"Yeah, they smell good, don't they?" said Lee in a hushed tone

We bought our hot dogs and Cokes, slowly climbed the stairs to the lower balcony and claimed three seats directly in the middle of the theater. It was about thirty minutes before show time and we enjoyed our snacks, tried on our 3D glasses and anxiously awaited what we thought would be the scariest movie we would ever see.

People continued to fill the many seats and then the lights slowly dimmed, signaling the show was about to begin. In the diminishing light, the statuesque maiden sculptures at each end of the balcony took on a ghostly appearance, adding to my already heightened anxiety about seeing my first 3D horror film. As the credits rolled, I carefully unfolded the 3D glasses, slid them over my eyes and gripped the armrests of my seat like a Louisville Slugger.

The stunning, 3D visual effects were complimented by deafening acoustics. Certainly, the technology did not compare to today's computer graphics animation, but I recall jumping out of my seat when the creature villain came crashing through a glass skylight and seem to land right in my lap. That was pure movie heaven to a twelve year old boy.

After the movie, we walked to the restaurant. Detroit's Flaming Embers Restaurant was an institution on Woodward at Grand Circus Park, where passers-by could watch flamboyant grill jockeys flip steaks as if they were conducting the Detroit Symphony Orchestra. I was able to order a T-bone steak, baked potato, salad and soft drink for just over a dollar. After ordering our meals, Lee, Frankie and I began accusing each other of closing our eyes during the scariest parts of the movies and laughed over who lied the best about not being frightened.

I relive that trip to the United Artist with great fondness and still remain amused at how much differently twelve-year-old boys view the world. While the Flaming Embers Restaurant was a downtown landmark and an exciting end to that evening, I would not consider it classy by my over-inflated standards of today. But on that memorable evening in 1957, no one could have convinced Frankie, Lee and me of that.

A Collage of Memories
By Melissa Hanna

When I try to recall the year of 1957, some things stand out in my mind. We had a prickly burgundy red horsehair couch. Heavy cording divided the back into three sections to match the loose seat cushions. There were large white lace doilies on each arm and across the three back sections. My Grand Mother spent hours tatting those doilies to specifically fit that piece of furniture.

The hoola hoop was the latest craze and the most popular toy of the Christmas season. We talked about this new toy endlessly and what you could do with it. All of us kids got one for Christmas.

The National Basketball Association franchise for the Pistons was purchased from some out of state, tier two circuit. The Detroit Pistons came into being and began their season at Olympia Stadium. All of our Fathers talked about this. I was finally old enough to wear pearls, a single pearl on a gold chain.

Every kid begged to be allowed to have Ovaltine in his or her milk. The Twin Pines Creamery delivered milk every morning to the house in glass bottles that were put in the milk chute next to the side door.

My father was extremely proud of the extravagant Christmas gift he gave my Mother that year, a full length beaver coat with wide lapels, three inch deep fold back cuffs and brown silk lining. In those days it was politically correct and stylishly chic to wear fur.

In 1957, Cousens Avenue was simply known as James Cousens.

The whole family went to an afternoon baseball game at Briggs Stadium. We sat in wooden seats with a big old-fashioned script "D" on the back.

One of our favorite games was hide and seek. We played in the alley because we could hide behind the metal garbage cans that were lined behind each house. Mr. Antonio's garage door was goal because it was in the middle of the block, opened on to the alley and was metal so you could hear when someone tagged in to goal.

We only played in the alley through Wednesday because the garbage trucks came down the alley to empty the tin cans on Friday and by Wednesday it got kind of stinky back there.

My father complained because the speed limit on the freeway was raised to 45 mph. A lot of people would object to traffic going that fast, he said.

My favorite song that year was; *Que Sera, Sera,*

"When I was just a little girl, I asked my mother, what will I be.

Will I be pretty, will I be rich, she told me tenderly; Que sera, sera.

Whatever will be, will be. The future's not ours to see. Que sera, sera".

A McDonald's hamburger was 14 cents.

When the family took a day trip to Belle Isle, the Aquarium was a wonderful afternoon experience. The majesty of the cascading water show of the Belle Isle fountain encouraged cars to drive the circular route around the elevated, lighted, stone-carved spectacle.

Barry Gordy Jr. founded Motown Records and started the Motown sound. That kind of music was going to corrupt young impressionable minds. We weren't allowed to purchase any 45s until my parents had listened to them first. We were only allowed to play the record player in the living room for one hour before dinner.

Stiff crinolines were the style under full skirts.

My first trip on the Boblo boat and to Boblo Island was the summer of 1957. For the trip to the island, we stayed on the top deck where it was noisy and windy. The entire family had their picture taken standing behind a huge wooden barrel that read Boblo Island. It was a giant park, surrounded by water and full of all kinds of rides.

In the fall, my Father raked the Oak and Maple tree leaves off of our lawn and mounded them on the grass between the sidewalk and the street. We loved to jump into the mounds of crisp, dry leaves. When the mounds got too high, the leaves were raked into the street and burned at the curbside. There is no other smell in the world like fall burning leaves.

This was the first year I was old enough to go Downtown on the bus with my mother for lunch on the mezzanine at Hudson's.

After school, we were allowed to play with the other kids on the block. Bucky Hagen's dad and Donna's father didn't get home from work until just before dinner. They lived across the street from each other so we always played ball in the street in front of their houses after school because there weren't any cars parked at the curb.

The rule was, we had to be home, on the front porch when the street lights went on. If we didn't make it on time, we had to sweep Mrs. Trudow's sidewalk the next week every day and nobody wanted to do it because she stood right out there to make sure you didn't miss anything.

Mrs. Trudow was a widow and didn't have a car. Every Tuesday and Thursday we took turns after school, two at a time walking with her to the local market, one block over and two blocks down. She always carried a black leather purse that had two straps. She would put both arms through the straps, folding her arms across her middle as she walked. Her black leather shoes with the wooden heels clicked on the sidewalk as she walked in front of us. We would try to match the pattern of her heels clicking as we followed behind.

We would wait on the bench in front of the market while she shopped. She would go in and buy us each a hard rock candy stick, bring it out for us to eat while we waited on the bench. Then when she finished her shopping, we would carry her two bags home for her. At Christmas, she gave each of us kids on the block who had carried her groceries a giant sugar cookie. She had baked them, wrapped each in white tissue paper with a fifty cent piece underneath the cookie. We were all impressed and felt very rich.

A First Class postage stamp cost 4 cents.

Just before Christmas, a couple of the families on the block decided to go to the Ford Rotunda to see the Christmas display.

Each family drove in their own car. I remember the hugest parking lot I had ever seen as we got near.

My father let the family off at a special area while he went to park the car. The road where we waited was paved with brick. The outside was very modern and us kids whispered about if we were at the right place.

As we walked in, we saw was the hugest Christmas tree we had ever seen with ornaments as big as our heads. There was a wide circular walkway with decorated trees on each side, no two alike. And live Poinsiettas everywhere. But the moving displays were really neat. Each one showed some different theme. There was lots of movement, lights and music. We waited in line a long time to see Santa (who had a real beard) He wore very soft fur on his coat, not scratchy like the coat of the Santa at Hudson's.

At the very end of the year, the Detroit Lions won the National Football League championship and everybody had high hopes for the next season.

When I think of 1957, these are the things that I remember.

Week-ends
By Betsy Rosinski

I remember in 1957, when we were just little kids and we lived in Detroit and went to St. Gregory's school. My oldest brother was a steel driver. He used to drive across the country in the big rigs, and when he would have a down time or when he would bring a load to Detroit, my mom would load the little ones in the car and we would go up to Michigan and Wyoming where all the truck drivers would bring their loads. We would pick him up and bring him back to the house. And my sisters came, my two older sisters who were married. One lived in Toledo and one lived in Monroe, and they had kids. I can't remember how many they had at that time, probably four or five kids apiece, and they would come up for Sunday dinner. We just had a little house in Detroit, it was only a two bedroom, but it was full when all these people came to visit. And my mom used to make fried chicken and we would just have a good time. She would make French bread, she baked bread and pies on Saturday when she knew everybody was coming. And we would make rolls. I remember standing there, helping her, putting those buns together. She made them like three-leafed clovers, so you had to do three balls at a time and stick them together and put them in the oven.

We used to have so much fun when we were little. One of my favorite things was when we would go on a mystery trip, that was fun. When we weren't having a Sunday dinner, Mom would say, "We're going on a mystery tour." She would put the four youngest ones in the car and we would go down to Carleton, where my Grandma lived. On the way down there she would pick up my aunt and her one daughter and we would go down through Sumpter. She would stop at this little store and she would get a loaf of bread, a bottle of Mustard and a pound of Bologna. We would stop along the roadside and we would have sandwiches. That was our mystery trip. We would visit with my cousin, we would run around, in the weeds and the woods. My mom and my aunt would sit there and they would have their bottle of beer. That was their trip. They would have a good time, and we had a lot of fun when we were little kids in 1957. I think that was the most memorable time for us.

Tiger Stadium
By Diana A. Hage

When I was a youngster of ten years old my Uncle Lee, who lived with our family to help with expenses in post-depression years, introduced me to baseball at Tiger Stadium. It was when very few people owned cars. We first took the streetcar to downtown Detroit. My most humorous memory was of my Uncle telling me to bend my knees so I wouldn't reach the "pay a fare" bar. Sometimes he got caught and sometimes he didn't but I was so embarrassed by this scene. Then we would transfer to another streetcar to reach Tiger Stadium. Incidentally, it was called Briggs Stadium at that time. I knew nothing about the game of baseball at that time so my dear Uncle Lee patiently pointed out all the mechanics of the game. He was ordinarily a quiet, soft-spoken man but when a game was going he could scream loud enough to be heard all the way to Michigan Avenue. He got me so hooked on the game that I knew all the baseball players in the American and National League. My most memorable game was one that lasted 24 innings when Al Benson, an ace relief pitcher, pitched more than twelve innings and then the game had to be called because of darkness as there were no lights then. After the games my uncle and I would walk down Michigan Avenue to catch the streetcar that took us home to the east side of Detroit. Sometimes he would stop at a bowling alley and bowl a game while I watched. I loved Tiger Stadium because it was pure, unadulterated baseball. The game was the focal point and not the commercialism that now surrounds most sporting events. We honored the American flag at the beginning of the game and then it was quiet concentration on the joy of baseball.

Clarence Comments
Memories from 1957 in Detroit
By Clarence Russell

Every summer my church, Vernon Chapel, would have an annual picnic day for the families of the church at Edgewater Amusement Park on 7 mile Road and Lasher. Back in those days Edgewater seemed so big. It did have a big wooden roller coaster, all the rides that we needed and carnival games galore plus a picnic area that the church would set up in for our family days. We would be there from noon till 8:00 p.m. It was normally held on Monday or Tuesday, the slow days for the park, so the church pretty much had the run of the place. The entire church went which was about 200 people. Actually I remember standing at the gate to Edgewater to direct the cars from the church as to where to park and the general public would come in and ask questions as if we worked there. My whole family would go my mother, father and brother. My favorite ride was the old wooden roller coaster.

I remember when you were going up the first hill the tracks were so warped and wavy that you wondered how the cars even stayed on the tracks. I never played any of the midway games. I remember going out in the morning and the carnival guy even showed me the trick to trying to toss the ring around the milk bottles and I still stood there all day probably 8 hours until I finally did it (of course it was free to me).

The other summer adventure was a ride down the Detroit River to BobLo Island which also had an amusement park, roller skating rink, a small zoo and a lot of other things to do. But the big thing with Boblo was the hour ride to and from the island, On the Columbia or St. Claire which were big boats you could sit around the outside rim and watch the river and people along the banks that were always waving to you. Or you could go to the second deck and watch people dance on the big dance floor. The third deck was for adults as the bar was up there so as a kid you had two decks to hang out on.

The third place to go for fun in Detroit was Walled Lake Amusement Park out in Walled Lake, Michigan. It didn't have as many rides as the other two but it did have the Walled Lake Casino which was a large dance pavilion overlooking the lake. That was always alive with music and people. Back then as a teenager it seemed like there was no end to the places you could go for fun. There were dances called sock hops at the Veterans Memorial Building on the Detroit River. Cobo Hall and the Great Lakes Insurance Building on Woodward had a large ballrooms in the basement for parties. Some of the night spots were Baker's Keyboard Lounge (still there), The Minor Key, The Twenty Grand that featured the Gold Room and The Driftwood Lounge. Back then Detroit was alive. It was fun to go out and just have fun.

BobLo and Walled Lake were usually family trips or with my friends families but the nice thing about Edgewater was that we could catch the Seven Mile Road bus from my house to Lasher and then we would walk the extra block. So that was our favorite place to go during the summer. The bus ride was a quarter and a transfer was a nickel. So I would cut grass on the weekends around my house and have enough money for the round trip rides and refreshments. Actually in the fifties most places you could go by bus.

The Minor Key was on Livernois and McNichols across the street from the University of Detroit. There was another club across the street from there that was an afterhours coffee shop that you could go listen to Jazz and drink coffee, no alcohol. It didn't open till 1:00 p.m. and stayed open until 6 in the morning. The Twenty Grand was on 14th at West Warren and was originally a 20 lane bowling alley with a bar. But there was a fire that completely burned it down. But they rebuilt at the same location, only when they rebuilt it the night clubs were the attractions and the bowling alley was just there.

The Driftwood Lounge was upstairs at the 20 Grand and was for Jazz and the older crowd .Downstairs at the 20 Grand was the Gold Room that was alive with the younger set, dancing to the tunes played by Frantic Ernie Durham, a local black DJ that had flaming red hair and would broadcast live from the Gold Room every night. The afterhours coffeehouse place was the Chessmate. A lot of famous people got their start there. Another thing I was remembering was Crowley Milner Department Store, downtown between Hudson's and Kern's. Kern's was famous for their big clock on the corner where everybody seemed to meet. Crowley's at Christmas had carnival rides on the 6th or 7th floor in the store. Another favorite place at Christmas was the Ford Rotunda in Dearborn with the Christmas Wonderland of animation and of course Santa.

Hudsons
By Greg Drake

Well, we loved going downtown to Detroit, it was a real treat for us. I was an only child. My parents had a grocery store and they both worked seven days a week. For us to actually have an opportunity to go downtown didn't happen that often, but when we did go down, my mother tried to make it something special. When my mom was going to shop we went down for the whole day. We would probably go down about 10 or 11 o'clock. We liked to stop at Stouffer's. That was a real treat for us, because it was on the way from where she used to park. We also used to go to Broadway Market, with their great, fantastic corned beef sandwiches. That was a real treat for us. They also had an absolutely fantastic restaurant at Hudson's. I thought it was fantastic at that time, but I was just a kid.

Mother always made sure that if we didn't eat at Stouffer's on the way in we would eat at the restaurant in Hudson's. They always had fantastic muffins. They just had great food, but I always looked forward to the muffins. My mother didn't make muffins at home, so anytime I could find good blueberry muffins or apple-nut muffins, I was always going to jump on that. We would have lunch down there and try to be home by dinner-time when my dad would get home from work about seven o'clock, so Mom could always cook a meal. That was one thing we didn't do, we didn't go out for dinner. We ate at home. It made it even more of a special day when we went downtown, we got to go to a restaurant and get waited on, which was kind of nice. And my Mom didn't have to do the dishes.

She had a couple of favorite places she liked to go in addition to Hudson's. But Hudson's was the big thing for her, that and Crowley's, which was right downtown. Hudson's, I think, was my favorite as a kid. I think my favorite place was the 12th floor, the toy store portion of Hudson's. We used to go up there, especially at the holiday time. You would go up there and they had huge Lionel train sets all over the place. They had a special room, just for trains. To me that was one of the things I looked forward to most over the holidays. But, I also wanted to look at the rest of the toys so we could figure out what we wanted for Christmas. That was a real special treat. They also had, at Hudson's, a stamp and coin store on the mezzanine that I was really intrigued by. I still have coin and stamp collections that I started there and I still have all the books that you opened up that you put coins in. Those things I bought there and we still have them. They are now in a safe deposit box, hopefully we have some coins that are worth something.

We walked around the store because Hudson's always had such fantastic windows. They had windows all around the outside of the store and they had those beautiful display windows. I remember, Mom and I walking around and looking in those windows in awe at some of the displays that they had. My mother was very fashion conscious, I think a lot of that she tried to pass along to me, not I am such a fashion-conscious person, but am at least I'm aware of it. Not that it is such a big deal, but I learned to like nice things. We didn't get much, but when we did get something, it was always very nice. Mom and Dad were always very good about that.

We used to buy stuff in there, at Hudson's. I never got to pick any Christmas presents, but my Mom would kind of watch to see what I liked and then Santa Claus might come along with that something. I never had a chance to pick them out, she just had that way of asking, "What do you like? What are you looking for?" Then something would show up under the tree. My Mother could take a hint real well, she knew. I'm not a very observant person, so I never would have known she was trying to do that in the first place. It was kind of fun, but that's my experience with Detroit Hudson's.

My mother used to like to go to Grinnell's to look at all the pianos and music stuff they had there. She actually enrolled me in a piano class. Way back then, Grinell's piano class was with a make-believe keyboard, it wasn't the real thing it was just a board, so you are there, thinking about music and you're looking at a black and white thing that doesn't do anything because its just a piece of paper. That seemed kind of unusual, but back then everybody didn't have a piano. So that was kind of different.

We enjoyed going to Bob-lo, which was a real treat. I probably was to Bob-lo, maybe four or five times in my life as a kid, with my cousins. We all lived in a row on Hannan Road, and there were six of us, boy cousins, and all of the aunts would go together. We had one spectacular time going to Bob-lo, we got to ride the Roller Coasters, Tilt-A-Whirls and all the other stuff that was there. It was a real fun experience, I think the biggest thing was going on the Bob-lo boat and that was a kind of really neat experience for us. We never had a chance to go out on a boat. I think I went one time on a date to Bob-lo Island, but that was just it. After that point in time it was more going out to a movie or a drive-in theater, going out to Big Boy's, Barhop's or Howard's Restaurant in Belleville. That's where we used to hang out once I got a Driver's License. We just hung around those places and the Wayne Drive-in and the Algiers Drive-in. We used to go on dates, to downtown Detroit. On a special date we would go down to see Cinerama, or go to the United Artists Theater. We had a favorite Chinese Restaurant, called Victor Lims, on Grand Circus Park. We used to go there on special dates and then go to a movie. The movies were spectacular, I mean, those movie theaters were just gorgeous. Cinerama was just fantastic, we would go downtown to see that at the Music Hall, or whatever it was called at that time, that was real treat because they had that huge screen that seemed like it wrapped all around the whole movie theater. That was fun!

Notes from Bill Szlinis
By Bill Szlinis

The restaurant that I think about was called "Greenfields" and it was on the lower level of a store. I can't remember exactly what store it was. I can remember going with my mother during the time we would go Christmas shopping. I just loved the place especially because I could get a scoop of mashed potatoes and gravy. The other restaurant I remember is Sanders, standing, waiting, trying to pick the right person or stool to stand behind, who looked like they were getting ready to finish their sundae or whatever they were eating. I do remember, close to fifty years ago, when I was working at Burton Abstract at 350 East Congress. We used to go to Greektown, before it was called Greektown, and there were the restaurants we used to go to. They would take us into the kitchen, the chef would open up the pot, take the lid off the pot and say, "This is what we have today." And that's when I got introduced to Greek food, as well as Lebanese food. That is how I got hooked on Kibbie Naha, which is raw lamb and wheat germ. And till this day I still enjoy it, but that's where I got introduced to it. Some of the attorneys at Burton Abstract were Lebanese and that was their big love. There was a restaurant, near Greektown called "The Shieks" and that was the place where we would go for true Lebanese food.

I remember going down to Vernor's probably in my later years of high school. In high school I went to the Catholic Central in Detroit, which was on Belmont right by the Cathedral. Occasionally we would get the bus or the streetcar and go down Woodward to Vernor's which was at the foot of Woodward, near the river, and have a Boston Cooler. A Boston Cooler was made with Vernor's and vanilla ice cream. That was a delight that only happened in Detroit. Lower Woodward Avenue, in addition to the Burlesque theater that I never got to go in, (by the time I was old enough they had torn it down) there were small shops. They also had novelty stores. They had magic tricks, itching powder, trick coins, squirting flowers, a lot of stupid little things like that young people really enjoy, I did too, and you don't see that stuff anymore. Went to Bob-lo, once or twice, and I really hated to see it change like it has today.

I remember going to Edgewater Park as kid and just hanging around. That was where I was introduced to French Fries, not with salt, but with vinegar and it just had a special taste, all of its own.

I worked at Edgewater Park when I was in school. I was in High School, my job was setting up the metal milk bottles that were knocked down by guys with baseballs. They had canvas all around it and we learned where to jump. I would get out of the way when they were coming up there. You could see some of the older guys who used to play baseball. They would think that they were Bob Feller, and they were going to break every bottle that they threw at, that didn't always happen. It was kind of an interesting Summer I spent.

We went to Walled Lake, I remember taking my wife out there and listening to and dancing to Johnny Green, it just escapes me, his famous song, it was something "down by the railroad track,. . . little old shack by the railroad track". There was also a dancehall in the Redford area around Greenfield Road. I can remember going there. We did a lot of dancing in those days.

I went to several games at Tiger Stadium and to this day I still think I have a picture of Virgil Trucks, they used to call him, "Double No Hit Virgil" because he had two no hitters in one season. Barney McCosky was a local hero for the Tigers because he grew up in the Springwells and Vernor area where my grandpa lived. Places around where my grandpa lived, in the Springwells and Vernor area, I can remember. St. Peter's church was in the Springwells and Vernor neighborhood. It was a Lithuanian Church I can remember going there a couple of times. My mother and dad were married there. The women sat on one side and the men sat on the other side, never together. When it was offertory time,

Father Savage would take off his vestments, grab a basket, and he did the collecting. Apparently when he did it there was much more in the baskets than when the regular ushers did it, he did a lot better than the ushers.

I don't remember the ethnic festivals, but I do remember the ethnic foods. My grandpa had a bar on Springwells near Vernor and every Friday we would go there and my aunt would make deep-fried Herring. That was the fish of the day and that was the best fish I can ever remember tasting. I don't think it was a Lithuanian recipe, it was my Aunt Della's recipe, anyhow. The Chamberlain Bakery was on Chamberlain and they had terrific sourdough and Lithuanian bread.

The theaters that I remember were the Redford and the Norwest, because that's where we moved out there in 1937. Dad built the house on Stout. When we moved out there it was a gravel road. We lived near Six Mile and Evergreen. It was the City of Detroit when we moved there, now it is called 'Redford'. The closest police station, when I lived in Redford, was at Schaefer and Grand River. My dad was a Detroit policeman and he worked at Precinct Number 12, which was at Seven Mile, near Livernois, the Palmer Park and Palmer Woods area. He used to take the Seven Mile road bus to work. I used to walk two and a half blocks to take the Six Mile Road bus when I went to Catholic Central and it was a fifty minute bus ride. Catholic Central was at Belmont and Woodward.

A Meeting Place Across Three Centuries – Campus Martius Park, Detroit

By Isaac David Kremer

Campus Martius when spoken of today elicits beautiful visions of Campus Martius Park, a legacy of Detroit's 300th birthday celebration, where concerts are held in the spring and summer, ice-skating in the winter months, and the constant thrum of pied-à-terre may be heard in the heart of Detroit's bustling office and commercial district. Those alive in the last years of the 1950s and who stood on this same spot would have witnessed what was in the 19th century the admitted center of the city, and a place which today is almost entirely gone.

The prototype for historic Campus Martius may be found in the European market square. For a brief period of time, here you could find within close walking distance a market, the City Hall, and cultural facilities like the Detroit Opera House which for the era in which it was built served a similar capacity to the cathedral for convening the many different people of the city together in one central location for important events and public gatherings without calling ones religious persuasion too much into question.

The generation largely responsible for creating this place was the same who returned bloodied and bruised from that great conflagration, the American Civil War. Among those who returned, certainly there was a hope to appeal to the "better angels of our nature" and create a culture that would nurture, foster, and support those democratic ideals and principles fought for, albeit through the brutal and often unfair arbiter of war.

So here in Detroit within a single generation, a series of impressive monuments and buildings sprang up. Starting with the French Renaissance styled Opera House with mansarded roof, this just as easily could have been in Paris than Detroit. How fitting that the generation which built this knew Father Gabriel Richard directly or by association, providing a direct connection to the French cultural tradition from which Detroit sprang from thanks to that intrepid Frenchman Cadillac in 1701.

A mansarded City Hall with Georgian cupola built in 1871, again included prototypical French features in the mansard evoking the libertie, equalitie, and fraternitie of another great democracy. The cupola may be seen as an effort to evoke the British tradition as well, for this was a dominant motif in building and design in the colonial era. Combination of these architectural features symbolized a compromise between the French, British, and American interests which occupied this ground at various times.

Wanting to honor the war dead, the artful Soldiers' and Sailors' Monument was added in 1872. Designed by sculptor Randolph Rogers, originally this four tier structure rose to an apex fifty-six feet in height. Bronze statues of eagles stand on the lowest tier; above them are figures representing Navy, Infantry, Cavalry, and Artillery branches of the U.S. Army, along with bas-relief monuments of Lincoln, Grant, Farragut, and Sherman. The third tier consists of allegorical female figures embodying Victory, Emancipation, History and Union. Local lore states that Emancipation is a depiction of Sojourner Truth who resided in Michigan and is buried in Battle Creek. At the peak stands an eleven-foot-high bronze Native American figure with sword and shield.

Taken together the Opera House, City Hall, and Soldiers' and Sailors' Monument represent a unified artistic object expressed in metal, brick, glass, and stone which appealed to the power of human reason and effort to overcome factional differences, rather than resorting to barbarism and open war. It is ironic that another generation itself returning from a great World War undid the progress these previous generations left.

Today only fragments from this era remain. The Soldiers' and Sailors' monument is the only one of the three monuments from this era to remain more or less intact. The monument was moved, rehabilitated, and incorporated into the present-day Campus Martius Park. More than anything else, Campus Martius across three centuries is a testament to the passage of time. And, while buildings long gone may be mourned, what is now in their place is just as true an expression of the hopes, ideals, and aspirations of this generation, just as what was there before expressed the same values of the generation which created them. Calling Campus Martius anything else would be a disservice to Detroiters today for whom the park and new buildings are a symbol of pride for a reemerging city and downtown and the unique culture that continues to create Detroit today.

Rambling Detroit with Rip
By F.X. (RIP) Coughlin

Where I lived it was a block and two houses on the Detroit side of Mack Avenue. So I would go up to Mack and then another block takes me to Charlevoix in Grosse Pointe and I could catch a Grosse Pointe Bus and you could not get off in the city until you got to Woodward and Jeff. That was the one place where the Grosse Pointe bus would pick up and discharge passengers until it got into the Pointes. So we would go there on the bus and walk up to Michigan Avenue and then walk up Michigan Avenue to what was then called Briggs Stadium. I cannot believe that it was only a quarter, but that's what is in my mind that it was. Because I remember 25 cents, seventy-five and ninety at three different periods as being the price for bleacher seats. So we would go in and see the Tigers for a quarter. The first few times I did it I was with three or four other guys, my grade school school-mates. Once or twice I just did it by myself. Which brings up the question, "You mean you would let kids do this by themselves?" The answer to that would be, "Yes." My family belonged to something called Turners which was on Jefferson Avenue. It was like a YMCA facility, a physical place, it had gyms, pools and that kind of stuff. It was a good five or six miles from where we lived on the East side. I remember walking that distance, for no good reason. I could take the bus, there were other ways I could get home. I was kind of a free spirit and I would walk it. It would take me the better part of an hour and a half or so. No one was ever going to find me if anything happened. There were five or six different streets that I could have taken that all ran parallel to each other. And, of course, you could have taken any of the other streets to ladder up to get up to the next one. There was no set route. Although, I will sheepishly admit that on one route there was a drug store where I would stop and look at the girly magazines. Although by today's standards they were barely PG. But, what the heck, it was a long time ago in a galaxy far away.

My mother was a school-teacher. I went to public schools one through eight and then I went to a Catholic high school. I knew at the time that there were huge differences between the Catholic school and the public schools. I became aware that the education in the public schools was different than the Catholics schools and it had nothing to do with religion. We were getting things earlier or more intensely than my friends in the public schools. I just figured that out later, although Detroit had a good public school system. But I firmly believe that during the 40s and 50s the teachers were teaching to their own children and during the 50s and 60s the demographics of the city changed and the teachers and administrators began to get tired and they just didn't work as hard as they had done. I definitely think that that occurred.

I also remembered being aware of the expressways. They were just being made in greater quantities. I remember the Southfield being built and parts of the North end of the Lodge being built, and how that was contributing to a phenomena that people were just beginning to realize of moving out to the suburbs. They had begun to learn that the purpose of building the expressways was to allow people to come into the city to get their places of employ. As it turned out it allowed people to get out of town and they took their employment with them. I remember taking the street cars, and I remember when they were sold to Mexico City, which I also think was 1957 or 58, something like that. I can remember earlier, my Grandmother taking me downtown, on the Detroit Street Railway.

I started to play football in '56, and the coach was, a lot of the time, talking about smoking. There were people on the street corners telling you that smoking was hazardous to your health, but everybody smoked and nobody paid attention to them. All the coach would say was that you didn't want to get started because it was bad for your wind. If I wanted to be a football player it was not a good thing. At that time, although I didn't smoke there was a lot going on behind garages. I do remember the conversations about cigarettes from the time we are talking about, the late 50s. Later we got into the Surgeon General's warnings and other things. And now we have smokeless everywhere and we have whole states smokeless.

The other thing I remember had mostly to do with cars. Friends down the street had a '57 Chevy Bel Air, the top of the line at the time. The Impala, I believe, came in 1958, as a product line. The Bel Air was real nice, but it also had a manual transmission. I remember neighbors that had '57 Chryslers, talk about gaudy, and fins that were unbelievable. But, the cars were incredibly fast. You didn't necessarily want to try to stop one or go around a curve. I can remember that we weren't anywhere near sixteen but that didn't keep us from taking Mom and Dad's car. Now, I never did cause my Mom and dad were very smart in that regard. I never got to drive the car. Hell, I never even got to start the car or pull it up the driveway. Other kids though, were being allowed to drive the car, so I wouldn't have been surprised that when their Mom and Dad were gone and the car was gone. I can remember being fourteen or fifteen, or less, being in cars with guys driving a 100 miles an hour in some of those well-powered Chrysler vehicles. Being an East-sider, it was much more a Chrysler area, than other areas of the city. Downriver you would find more Fords and on the North side there would be more GMs. It was kind of an interesting era, but it was the manual transmissions that I specifically remember regarding the '57 cars, by the sixties you just didn't see them anymore. An interesting thing about '57; it was a joke at the time about how gaudy the cars had become, especially about the fins. We had tri-color Chryslers, one of which I remember, not so fondly, was gray and black and white. Another was coral, black and white. How you could find enough room inside all the chrome to get three different colors? '57 was about the peak in the height of fins and the amount of chrome.

It was just about the late Fifties that I became aware that in the South there was significant, I didn't know what the word, "segregation" meant. I would see pictures in the newsreels and stuff, colored fountains and other signs of discrimination. As a kid who had only had a Catholic education, by this time I had been in school for eight years, it did not make any sense. I honestly couldn't understand, since I knew the South not necessarily to be Catholic, but to be Christian. I never could understand how they could reconcile how they lived with what they were taught. It wasn't too long after that the Civil Rights movement started, then it dominated the next years, if you will. But I remember in the late fifties being confused, more by the reaction that there wasn't more rebellion, but more by the action of the whites because I didn't know how they came to the conclusion that these were the right answers.

There was something I thought about. It had to do with the role of China. I can specifically remember being taught that although China was a large part of the globe and a lot of people lived there, it didn't exist. How the state department managed to convince the entire country that we can ignore this much of the planet, I don't know. It seemed to emanate from the Federal government. I remember having these thoughts, that China was unimportant because it didn't exist because we had political differences. It was unnecessary to know anything about China, because it was unimportant.

I remember when "Under God" was put on our currency, it seemed it was either 1954 or 1956. I asked one of the Nuns, I thought that she would think that this was important because we were a good Catholic school and all. And she said, "No, all it is an affirmation of something that you know to be true." I also remember there didn't seem to be a lot of conversation about it.

Mary's Memories
By Mary Herring

In 1956 we moved to Michigan. We spent our recreation time as children, doing two of my favorite things; roller skating on the sidewalks with the old steel-wheel and key roller skates that you attached to your shoes. And then there were a couple of years where we built the stilts, the walking wooden stilts. We walked everywhere in town on stilts. Those were two of my fondest memories, growing up, as a child, those activities with my friends.

The other thing that I remember that I really enjoyed was playing with my dog. I had a dog, named Bimbo, it was just a mutt, but he and I went everywhere together. I was kind of a loner as a child because I was the fourth child of four children. The closest to me in age of my siblings was my sister who was six years older. So when I was growing up, my siblings were off to college out-of-state and inaccessible. So I spent a lot of time playing by myself. I was a tom-boy and so I loved the out of doors, as I still do, and I spent many, many happy hours, just playing by myself and my dog and whoever else would come along with me. I looked for adventure wherever I could find it, and I usually found it. I had a vivid imagination, I used to love to run, skip and sing. I used to love trees, and still do, and I used to sing as I walked down the sidewalk, and I would hug a tree and sing to it. If people didn't think I was crazy I'd still do that to-day. I was very much of a nature lover so I loved playing outside. I used to play 'Jacks', loved 'Jacks' and got quite proficient at them actually. I don't remember what year it was, it seemed around the time I was ten years old,

I think it was the time the 'Slinky' came out, coils of wire and they would fall down the steps. Growing up, when we moved to Michigan, I went to a Catholic school from fifth through eighth grade, walked to school which wasn't far from where we lived. And, at recess, we'd play marbles, baseball with the nuns, hop-scotch, and jump-rope. Those childhood games that didn't cost much and weren't electronic brought great joy. We played on the playground equipment. I lived in a new subdivision. The first two years that we lived there we rented a house. At that house there were huge trees which I climbed all the time. I spent more time in trees when I was a teen-ager and a pre-teen, than I did on the ground. We had a huge barn on that property that was converted to a garage. It had an old hay-mow, a loft above, and myself and my girl-friend put an old bedspring up in the loft and we would sleep out there in the Summer. We dodged the bats that roosted in the loft. It had an open door that would have been used to store feed in the old days, that we would look out and open at night to watch the stars. We read comic books by flashlight, under the bed sheets, when we were dodging bats.

I have a scar on my chin to show from those times, because I fell on the cement floor, coming down one night and got six or eight stitches in my chin. My dad walked me about three blocks to the doctor's office and they stitched me up, that's the only childhood injury that I remember.

As, I said, I went to a Catholic school from fifth to eighth grade and we children used to help Father Tom Collins, our parish pastor, with activities. The eighth grade girls even helped him do his bookkeeping. That was before the Catholic priests had all the fancy staff they have now, they utilized the children. And we were in the church choir and the Altar Boys did those duties that Altar Boys have. I went to Edgewater park a couple of times. It was a treat that our parish priest gave us. Every year, Father Tom Collins, in appreciation for what we school children did for him and for the parish, took us to Edgewater Park, as a treat. I remember three years I went toward the big city of Detroit and I enjoyed the many amusements at Edgewater Park. It is still a very vivid memory, that huge, wooden roller-coaster that they used to have, before the modern days of roller-coasters. That was great fun. There were three classes, probably a total of maybe fifty or sixty of us that went. We filled up one school-bus.

My parents were charter members of the Devil's Lake Yacht Club in Irish Hills and we had a cottage at Devil's Lake. Every Summer we would spend quite a bit of time staying at the cottage. My Dad could only be there on week-ends because he would be working during the week. Mom would take us kids and we would stay at the lake. My recreation, again because I was kind of a loner, was to go out in the little rowboat, taking my fishing line and my dog, and spend several hours on the lake fishing for Perch, or whatever I could get. 'Course we enjoyed swimming. One of my favorite activities was fishing for Crayfish or crabs, in the rocks. What we did was tie a piece of raw bacon to the end of a string, put the string down between rocks at the shoreline, wait for that Crayfish to sense that he had something on the line. He would grab and hold on to it, and never let go and I would pull him out of the rocks. I put him in a bucket until I collected as many as I felt like that day and then I would put them back and start all over the next day.

But, getting back to the lake, my father and mother were interested in sailing with the Devil's Lake Yacht Club. They had a fleet of Lightning sailboats which usually took a three man crew and every Sunday during the Summer months they had sailboat races. If I wasn't in a boat with my siblings, I would be helping my Mom and Dad in the Race Committee boat, or swimming at the Yacht Club with my friends. Lake activities in the summer were a large part of my life. We continued to go back, even after the cottage was sold, until my parents passed away. At Devil's Lake there was a roller rink that used to be a dance hall where my parents had seen Louis Armstrong there when they were a young couple, and Ozzie and Harriet Nelson and some of the big names of the time. The dance hall was just down the street from us at the lake. Manitou Beach had a grocery store and a Merry-go-Round, and you could ride that Merry-go-Round as long as you wanted for a dime. The old dance hall became a Roller Rink so we utilized that, I roller-skated a lot as I was growing up, either on the sidewalks or inside a building. When I was a teenager, they converted it to a dance hall again.

In Tecumseh, they had an old theater and in the late fifties we could go to the movies on Sunday afternoon and you could get in for 15 cents, so we could go and see a movie, as a treat, Mother had to approve it first, of course. That's how I would spend my allowance money, going to the movies.

I remember my Dad was an avid card player, so was my mother, so he taught us to play Poker when we were young children. He taught us to play Chess when we were children, of course he taught us Checkers, Chinese Checkers, all those wonderful games that we had when were growing up. Mother taught us to play Cribbage, I still play it, Pinochle, Euchre, all those fun things that you can interact with people while playing. We learned those games quite young and played a lot with each other. We didn't have a sewing machine that I remember so I would make my own doll clothes and sew them by hand when I was at the age of eleven or twelve. That would have been about 1957.

I think recreation, back then, at least in my family, was much simpler. We didn't necessarily have to go some place far away. We used what we had at hand, money was tight. My Dad was a salesman, and he worked on commission, when money didn't come in you couldn't go too far down the road to find recreation elsewhere. We did a lot of things that didn't cost a lot of money, they just took some imagination.

The Woodward Avenue Experiences
By Charles Van

We went to the Detroit Main Library often on the city bus. It took two transfers, which meant catching three different buses from our house but we could be there in a little over two hours. We would sit in the seat that held three people: my Mother, my little brother and I.

The time went by very quickly. As soon as we settled into the wide leather seat, Mother would always ask, "What are you interested in finding out about today?" We would then try to figure out what part of the library the Dewey decimal system card file would tell us to go to. We each signed out only two books at a time because we had to be able to carry them home and back ourselves.

I am sure Mother had told us about the Diego Rivera murals before but in the spring of 1957, we signed out a book about the artist and took it home to read and talk about. The photographs in the book showed a large man. He had dark intense eyes and in every picture looked angry or upset. I didn't understand much about his politics. The book said many of his earlier works were mostly about that.

My brother and I were really interested in the murals we saw at the Main Library though. There was a lot of gray. But sharp colors drew our attention to different areas. The book said the subject was the celebration of the Assembly Line. We were most interested in the people though. Many of the men had round faces that reminded us of the pictures of Diego Rivera in the book. And some of the people had dark skinned faces. Many of the people's bodies were at unusual angles. It looked like it would be hard to work given the positions they were standing in. But maybe they wanted to say something?

When I looked at the murals, I could almost hear the machines. It was easy to imagine lots of motion.

Looking at the murals and reading the book made us want to know more about factories and assembly lines.

Those murals told us a story. We didn't fully understand the story at the time but even then, what we saw made us think, made us ask questions. Over the years, we would remember how impressed we were with the murals and the messages our young minds received.

Directly across the street from the Main library was the DIA. (Detroit Institute of Arts) On one of our bus adventures, Mother walked us across Woodward. There was a very famous exhibit that had come to Detroit that she thought we should see. I don't remember anything about the exhibit but I do remember the DIA. I would always remember that first visit.

Our first impression as we walked inside was of lots of shiny pink and orange stone and very dark polished wood like we saw at the Henry Ford Estate. There were a lot of steps. Each flight of steps led to a different experience. The Renaissance art, the French chapel, ancient Egypt and the Pharaohs. And seeing an actual sarcophagus was surrealistic. Just so much to take in. And then we walked down a flight of rough stone steps to a European outdoor café right in the middle of the building. (indoors)

After that first DIA experience, my brother and I were hooked. We would find books at the Library and ask Mother to take us across the street to the DIA to see or find out more on different topics. I think she realized we were just looking for reasons to go back to the DIA. But she never told us so.

Memories
By Keith Bruder

We didn't go down town a lot until later on, when I was older, when we really got into the sixties. I remember a lot of things about around here in Western Wayne County before that. One thing that happened in the late fifties, my first father had died of heart trouble when I was seven. My mother remarried in 1956. I wondered later, "Would I be ready to step into a ready-made family of four that went from nine to seven, five and three? I always felt fortunate that someone would want to step up to be our father." We lived on a small farm on Elwell road, about one-half mile from Huron River Drive. All of that area south of the Expressway and the Huron River basically was made up of farms, it was very heavily agricultural. They were small, seven to twenty acre farms, we had a seven acre farm. My step-dad had a milk route. I enjoyed riding around to the farms in southern Wayne County and Eastern Washtenaw County to pick up the cans of milk. The farmers would have two sets of cans, they were maybe 25 gallon cans, or 15 gallon cans. Every day, my step-dad would go by and pick up a set of milk cans and take it to the creamery in Detroit and pick up another set of cans. You would then bring those cans back, they were always dropping off one set and picking up another. Many times I would go with him. You got to know all of the farmers, the immigrant farmers and the Polish farmers who settled southwest of here. He later sold the milk route. Little did he know that was not a good time, because right away he could not find a job. The reason he sold the milk route was that the State of Michigan determined that they wanted to change the sanitary requirements on milk. A new law went into effect that prohibited canned milk. You had to buy stainless steel, refrigerated bulk tanks. They were very expensive and some of the small farmers he picked up the cans for, having one can every other day, obviously could not afford it. That's when he said, " It's time to quit."

What I remember, in that period of time, was the agrarian, agricultural parts of Wayne County. My Grandfather, in Sumpter, had a 120 acre farm that was a dairy farm. I would go over there in the Summer-time for a week or two week periods and help out. At the end of the year, he said, "You like that little Holstein calf. That's your pay for the Summer." I knew that all I was able to do for him was to get in the way, but he gave me this little Holstein calf. I would go over and see it all the time, later it had a calf. Something happened to my calf, physiologically or biologically, so it couldn't have calves anymore. So my Grandfather sat me down and said, "Now Keith, everything on a farm, outside of cats and dogs, has got to pay for its keep." "I understand that," I said. So we loaded the cow in the 1955 Dodge one-ton stake truck with the live stock racks on it and took it to the Detroit livestock yard, and sold it. So here I am eleven years old and going on 12, and I got two hundred and twelve dollars for that cow. For a young boy in those days $212 was a lot of money.

A few months later I overheard my Mom and Dad talking about him liking to have a tractor, as soon as he saved up enough money to buy a used tractor. The used tractor was going to cost $450 for a 1947 International H tractor with cultivators and a two bottom plow. So, I said, " Dad, I've got $212 in the bank so, if you want to go into partners, we can get a tractor." We used the tractor for years, farming there on Elwell road, and I still have the tractor. After my Dad died, we sold the farm and my Mom said I should have the tractor since I was a partner.

In 1958 two things happened that changed our life. Off Elwell Road, where I lived there was developed Lauren Court, which filled with houses and Dr. Alford divided his sixty acres to build houses along Elwell Road. It was kind of like the first wave of suburban sprawl. But, for me, it was great because it brought a lot of other kids into the area and now there was always someone to play with. So there was always someone to play hockey, always someone to pick up for football or baseball.

In 1958, the Van Buren school system built some new schools. I thought it would be great to go to a new school, since one was being built on Elwell Road.   But, we lived on the wrong side of the tracks to go there, we lived North of the rail road tracks so I went to Rawsonville school. I went to Belleville school for the Kindergarten through fifth grade, but was going to Rawsonville for the sixth grade. Rawsonville school, as most know, was built by Henry Ford. It was a two story building. I was in the sixth grade, the sixth grade at Rawsonville was in the basement.

Several years later, I was reading to prepare for a talk to the local historical society, on Henry Ford and the influences of Henry Ford on the area of Belleville, Sumpter , Ypsilanti and Van Buren Township. Henry Ford contributed a lot of money to build the original Rawsonville School. Two or three months before the dedication of that school, Ford was over by Ecorse Road. He had stopped where he saw a mowing machine, a hay mowing machine. He stopped and there was a young boy, playing in the yard.

"Young man," Ford said, " Do you know if that mowing machine is for sale?"

"Well, sir, I don't know," replied the boy, " but it is my Dad's and I will check."

"I would appreciate it," concluded Ford.

A few weeks later, at the dedication of the Rawsonville school, Henry Ford was there. He walked up to the boy and asked, " Did you find out about that mowing machine?"

" Yes sir, but my Dad doesn't want to sell it."

"O.K." said Ford.

But the boy continued, " May I introduce you to my mother and father?"

So a young boy, about 8 years old, introduced his parents to Henry Ford.

When I went to the high school they were in the process of building. I remember my music class was held in an old building, like a wood-framed house, a medium-sized house, without any interior walls, and that was our music room. That's where we learned to play a Tonette and later went to a Saxophone with Mr. Coffelt as our teacher. They called them, back then, Tonettes. Now, they are called Recorders.

Rawsonville road was gravel, it had to be gravel because the incline was so steep that without gravel you wouldn't be able to get up in the Winter. On the West side of Rawsonville Road was a pond, of captured water from springs on the hillside. The pond was quite large and parents would bring their children there to go ice skating because it was a great pond. It was probably the size of a football field, maybe bigger.

I used to go with my Father, in the Spring, when there used to be a lot of Smelt in the river. I don't know if they ran up the river or down the river. We would dip for them below Ford Dam, in that stretch of the Huron River before Rawsonville Road. There would be a lot of people dip-netting for Smelt. We would go down there at night and there would be dozens of people. A Smelt is a real small fish, maybe the size of your thumb, maybe six inches long and the diameter of your thumb. I guess they run at night, I don't know why but I have always seen them fishing at night. They were a small fish. It was not much to clean them, really. You would get like a gunny-sack full, or maybe two gunny-sacks, at night. You would clean them and then freeze them and later cook them by the dozens. They were so small, basically you would just clean the insides out and normally eat them – old-timers, like my Dad would eat them bones and all, they were so small and crunchy. I usually picked the meat off of both sides and didn't eat the bones, I guess I had a phobia of bones getting caught in my throat. It was something a lot of people did – it was something that happened on the lake.

Also, along the lake there were a number of gravel pits, we used to go over to them and get road gravel, which was a mixture of sand and stone to put in the driveway. On certain sides of the lake, depending upon the curvature of the lake there would be sand and gravel deposited in other places silt.

The big event in the Spring, along with Smelt fishing, would be the gravel roads. When the frost came out of the ground they were awful. I don't know if it was the high water table or what, gosh, some years it would be a quagmire. We lived on a gravel road, one-half mile off of a paved road. Some years we had to park at the paved road, because you could not get down the gravel road. For someone who has never lived in the country, they have always lived in the city, they can't understand what dirt roads are like when they drop out. I have seen School Buses, gravel trucks. County trucks, and Road graders drop right down, and they weren't going anywhere. It was kind of fun. After I bought that little International H tractor, (maybe I started my entrepreneurial career a little young) I would park the tractor in front of the house with a chain on it. People would knock on the door, " Hey, could you pull out our car?" "Yeah, O.K. it will be two dollars." I would pull them out and I had made two dollars in just a few minutes.

The Roller Rink in Sumpter, at Willis and Sumpter, was always a great place to go as a kid. Parents would take you there on a Saturday afternoon, or maybe a Friday night and leave you for a while so you and they could have fun. It was kind of a special treat down there. The rink is still there, I'm not sure what hours it is open.

We had a little League program here when I was growing up. They didn't have T-Ball or some of those programs they have to-day, they had Little League then Babe Ruth and Connie Mack. I played while in High School. I played on the Yankees. We won the pennant one year. The only reason I remembered this was that they gave me a trophy. That year I played first base and I batted .636. No home runs, one triple, one double and lots of pathetic singles that dropped just over the Shortstop.

We were in 4-H. At that time the 4-H Fair was going stronger than it is today. The 4-H Fair started when Henry Ford died. All that land was owned by Henry Ford, he owned about 300 acres around Belleville. Henry Ford had a farm north of the Expressway and after he died it became the Wayne County 4-H Fairgrounds. We took sheep and showed sheep there. That was fun. We would take our vegetables and our corn and our Winter projects. You would always work on Winter projects, like basic wiring, like wiring a lamp and little carpentry projects. It was so you could learn to handle tools. Those were the Winter projects and we would have a Winter show. Usually the Winter 4-H show was down at Huron High School, in the gymnasium there. The Summer show, obviously, was the 4-H Fair at the Fairgrounds. You would bring your crops, your vegetables, canning, and then you might be given ribbons. One year I got Grand Champion Pig for a hog I had, I was the only entry. After that more kids started raising hogs. We usually took sheep over to the 4-H Fair.

We used to play Hockey on Belleville Lake. I would say it was the worst place in the world to play Hockey. Back then the ice would get quite thick, as it cracked, you could look down and see a foot deep or more, maybe. We used to play right here off of Liberty Street. It was the worst place to play Hockey, because someone would take a slap shot and it might go a half a mile. "O.K., you hit it. You go get it." Then you had to go and get the puck and bring it back, while every body else sat down and rested. There were also many ponds behind the homes along Elwell road on the small farms where we could always play Hockey.

Back then you could get a motor scooter with less than eight horsepower. Anything greater than eight horsepower was classified as motorcycle and required a license. We went to Detroit and bought a used Cushman scooter. It had little, twelve-inch wheels with fat tires. It was an awkward thing, a big, heavy thing. It was the most unsafe thing in the world. It had two speeds, on the tank. You had to take one hand off of the handle bar to shift gears while using a pedal for the clutch and the other hand to control the speed. I always said, it had two speeds; slow and slower. You could barely hit 35 miles per hour downhill, with the wind. But it was about all that was around. There were two or three of us who used to ride around on scooters over to Willow Run Airport. We would go to the restaurant over there, get a Coke or something. That was three miles away, *that* was a long ride.

Lions of the Night
By Ken Askew

The Detroit Lions championship team of 1957 has been documented in gallons of ink over the years as writers glorified their exploits on the gridiron. Hundreds of thousands of Detroit fans cheered them to victory. Hundreds more were followers of the antics of the players after they left the locker room and roamed the city. It was a sport not documented by statistics and many times not suitable for documentation but it was a favorite pastime of many.

The observation of the behavior of the Lions players was a form of entertainment across the community. Stories of the Lions exploits after hours were a staple topic of conversation. Much of it was good-hearted humor like Les Bingaman picking up the back of a Volkswagon in the Sports Car Ypsilanti showroom to impress Leon Hart who was seriously considering becoming a VW dealer. Four Lions in a VW did not dissuade Hart from the enterprise.

Mostly the Lions were tracked from bar to bar across the city for that was their preferred habitat from Kelly's and the Lamp Lighter on the far West to the Lion's Den or the Flame, or even the Long Branch. In Bobby Layne's words, from his book, <u>Always on Sundays,</u> "One thing that has always puzzled me is the reaction of people when they see an athlete out on the town. If you walk in the front door, check your coat and go to the bar like everyone else, it only takes 10 minutes for the word to get all over town that Bobby Layne's down at the Long Branch, hymn-singing drunk".

It was seldom necessary for any Lion to buy a drink, as crowds formed to help them with their evening partying. Lions on the loose were avidly hunted in the nightspots. It was the sport of the fan to track them down and buy them a drink. Men loved to rub shoulders with the heroes of Sundays and women loved to brush against the muscles of the famous. Some of it was reciprocated.

In all honesty it must be admitted that there probably were Lions who went home to their loving wives and family, but they were seldom sought by admiring fans. It was the carousing crew that was usually led by Bobby Layne that helped create the legends of the Lions of the night. Frequenting the night spots while other football teams were handcuffed by bed checks and curfews, the Lions roared. They gained the loyalty of many Detroiters. Some of the legends relate to the protection the Detroit police gave to the players. Legend has it that the police formed a protective cordon along Mt. Elliot when a favorite player was expected to leave and head toward his Jefferson Avenue apartment. They made sure that no innocent Detroiter might be involved with interference of a player.

Perhaps the most outstanding legend, considered fact by many, was the famous trial of Bobby Layne when he was accused of drunken driving. The golden-haired, handsome hero was placed on trial before a jury mostly composed of women. The party-line was that the prosecution feared unfair prejudice if men were allowed. The arresting officer gave his testimony with the salient points of the charge being that the defendant had an aroma of alcohol on his breath, slurred his speech and staggered when he walked.

When the attorney for the defense took over he called Layne to the stand. "Is it true," he asked, " that you had alcohol on your breath?"

"Yes," answered Layne, " I had been in a bar and been offered drinks by a number of fans. Being polite I appeared to drink with each of them while only taking a tiny sip to make them feel good."

"The officer has testified that your speech was slurred when you were arrested. What is your response to that?" the defense attorney asked.

"Well, shucks," replied Layne, "At the University of Texas, where I went to school, almost ever one spoke like me. I think that the officer just ain't familiar with a Texas drawl."

The testimony about Layne staggering was dealt with in the defense summation when the attorney recited the number of times Layne had been sacked, knocked down, manhandled and injured while he was upholding the honor of the city and gaining the reputation of one of Detroit's heroes. A few of the lady jurors seemed to weep openly, while others clasped their hands to their chests. Bobby was found not guilty.

Whether the stories were true or part of the mythology that always seems to hover around individuals that are destined for greatness and immortality for their achievements, the presence of the Lions in the city created a pastime of Lion-watching. The watchers were well rewarded.

They were a splendid group of athletes, those Lions who played to a Championship and they were an amazing group of men who were the Lions of the night. In Layne's book, Joe Schmidt perhaps summed it up best when he said, "We weren't a bunch of guys who were holy guys. We were young guys, and young guys are young guys when they get together."

Professional Women's Pastimes

By Mildred Artley

Things happened in the fifties, things like Bob-Lo. We used to go on the Bob-Lo boat. Here is the Henry and Edsel Ford Auditorium that they built downtown right next to the river. I first heard the Boston Pops at the Ford Auditorium. The Masonic Temple in Detroit is the largest Masonic Temple in the United States. It was an opulent building, they had rooms for all kinds of things. When my brother-in-law graduated from Law School of Wayne State University, they had the Graduation exercises there. They had a lot of public functions there, plus, they had a stage. They had stage plays or outside performers come there.

There are the historical churches. I have been on the tour of Detroit. You get the tour out of the Historical Museum, they handle it. There used to be a Western Market, but they disbanded it, but Eastern Market is still going. I have been there many times, to Eastern Market. There is the old Mariner's Church that is down next to the entrance to the tunnel. I visited the Edsel Ford home and the Henry Ford estate at Fairlane in Dearborn. I went to the Franklin Cider Mill out in Franklin Village. The town that time forgot, they called Franklin Village.

I went to the Detroit Institute of Arts. At the Detroit Institute of Arts, in the late fifties, they had programs there which were called, "Brunch with Bach". After church we would drive down there, to the Institute, and you went through the food line, it was in the outdoor food court. This was in the Summer, and every Sunday they had a different musical group. It could have been a brass or string group, piano or vocalist. The idea was that you went through the lunch line and got your lunch , then you sat at the tables there for an hour or an hour and twenty minutes and you heard all this music that they called, "Brunch with Bach." What was interesting was that it was the beginning of serving food with plastic tableware. They had plastic cups, plastic plates, plastic flatware and paper napkins. They didn't want the noise of glasses made out of glass, and they didn't want the noise of metal flatware and ceramic plates so they had gone to plastic and paper. Also, at that time, George Perrault had come into notice with his world travel pictures. On the back side of the DIA they have an auditorium near the back entrance. That was a popular place to go when they had programs periodically. I don't know if it was every two or three weeks they would have a different one of his shows, but it was a popular place to go. And that was at the DIA.

Across the street, North of the DIA there was the Old World Market. There was a building there, I think created originally for immigrants coming in to Detroit from other countries, to live. They had activities there for them, they had places where they could learn the English language. It was kind of educational. Once a year they had a festival there and they would have different rooms set up with different ethnic foods and we would have dinner at one of them. Then you went into the auditorium and they put on a program where the different ethnic groups would perform, in costume, their native dances. They had magicians and musicians, all kinds of clogging and dancing. I always went with somebody to the DIA. It was a nice event.

I was working out at Willow Run. During the war years, 1941 to 1946, I worked for Bendix Aviation in Wayne. They made propellers until the war ended. It was a company from Fort Wayne, Indiana. When the war ended they brought us applications for jobs out at Willow Run because Kaiser – Frazier was coming in. We all filled out papers, so many of us left work at Bendix on Friday and Monday morning reported out to Willow Run. I became acquainted with a bunch of girls at Bendix and then at Willow Run I became acquainted with a lot more people, women especially. On Monday night we would usually go downtown shopping after work. We got out of work and drove downtown because all of the stores were open on Monday nights. They also were open on Saturday, we usually went shopping on Saturday, but we always went on Monday night. We would have dinner and shop. Knowing all these girls, they all had interests, some of them were from Detroit and I became acquainted with all these places to visit.

I remember historic Fort Wayne, at Jefferson and Livernois, I visited there. One of my friends had a boy who went into the military and that is where he had to report. Fort Wayne was where they were taking the men from the greater Detroit area. In the fifties, Fort Wayne was kind of a ghost town. It had been vacated, the buildings left to deteriorate, the ground had grown up to grass and weeds, like hay. Apparently, Fort Wayne was popular, maybe during World War I. I'm not sure about that. But, there are some beautiful brick homes there where all the officers lived with beautiful grounds that they maintained and an underground pit where they had guns. Henry Ford's Greenfield Museum and Village was popular in those years and I made many, many trips there. Years ago they had live theater productions on Sundays and we went there to quite a few of them.

Over in Canada we went to Jack Miner's Bird Sanctuary. We would drive over there and have dinner and then go and see the Canada geese. We went over there, of course on Sundays and there wasn't a great deal open there because they were religious people. You could see the birds and you could see them feeding the birds, but none of the other little activities they had there were open. We always enjoyed going over there, there was always some nice place to eat in the Windsor area. Of course it was exciting going through the tunnel. Lots of cities have tunnels, but I don't know of many that have a tunnel that connects two countries, like we have.

Then we get to entertainment. The first one that comes to mind is the Fisher Theater. That was in the Fisher Building and that was one of the most elegant buildings ever built in Detroit. You go in the Lobby and it has this mosaic ceiling. The first floor was real active, with all of these beautiful shops. There were dress shops. Of course everything was very expensive. Beautiful linen stores, beautiful men's stores with all kinds of men's clothing. They had restaurants, there was the Pegasus. That was Greek food. They had real good food there and it was one of the popular eating places when we went to the show. If you went in there before you went to the theater, you could order drinks. Then at Intermission time you went down there and they would have your drinks ready for you. They had names on the glasses, they knew who they were for. You had time to drink your drink and get back up the stairs for the second half of the program. They had a nice bookstore there, they had a couple nice art galleries. In addition to all that they had the theater, the Fisher Theater, and they are still open there, the Fisher Theater is still there. Also in the downtown are was another theater, the Hillberry Theater. That was at Wayne State University. We used to go there to a lot of their plays, in the evening. Orchestra Hall was also a place we went. Sometimes the Symphony played there but sometimes they had plays.

We got into night life. Greektown used to be a popular place to go. All along the street there were Greek restaurants. If you liked Greek food, that was the good place to go downtown.

We went downtown to the Flower Show. The Flower Show was a big event in Detroit and it ran for a week. You could go there and spend several hours because it was a real spacious thing. All the florists and all the people that had greenhouses would have big displays. All of it was live, all the sod, they brought in, and all the trees and flowers. That was an annual event that we went to frequently. At Eastern Market, again, that's the Farmers Market. They always had their flower show every year, usually in May when they would sell all their annual flowers. We used to go down to that because there were also places to eat. It seemed like there was always a restaurant that we wanted to go to, when we went to these places downtown. We even went to the International Strawberry Festival in Hamtramck. Hamtramck has a Polish Festival every year. We went there as a group of girls from work to one restaurant that we always ate at. Sometimes some of my friends from Belleville went with me. I always drove, because I knew the West side of Detroit. I didn't know the East side of Detroit, but I knew the West side pretty well, and I didn't mind driving. When we went Downtown, I was always the designated driver.

The Michigan State Fair was an annual event. We went there because they had, either a prominent band, singer, or some star from Hollywood in the Coliseum. Of course, they always had the horse-shows and the circus. That was an annual thing, to go to the State Fair, just as there has been the Thanksgiving Parade.

Some of the hotels and motels come to mind. The first one is the Botsford Inn. That was out Grand River. The Botsford Inn was owned for a time by Henry Ford. He developed it. It was an old inn that had been a way-station for stage-coach travelers.

It had all the original floors and it was filled with antiques, but it was a lovely eating place, a busy place. It was a lovely place to go for a Sunday dinner.

I became acquainted with a girl at work, she worked with me and then she moved to Ford's. She worked for Ford, in the offices. She belonged to the Ford Motor Girls Club. It was an organization of the office girls that worked for Ford Motor Company, in all the installations in the Detroit area. They were highly organized. They had a meeting every month at the Ford World Headquarters down there on Michigan Avenue in Dearborn. And they always had a program. They always brought in outside entertainment. They had a couple parties out at the Botsford Inn. They rented the whole facility and had tents set up outside for the entertainment.

Chrysler also had a Women's Organization for the women that worked in their offices, not the women who worked out in the shop or factory, these were the office workers. There was also a Dodge one that I knew of. I don't know if there was a General Motors one, but I presume they might have one. Ford Motor was a very active one. I went because my friend belonged and I always went as a guest, but then they made me an honorary member. I've got a little card they gave me, because I was always a participant. They did a lot of community service. At Christmas time they had the dolls that they dressed for the Goodfellows. They would have thousands of them lined up in that office building. They built racks and they had a judging contest. They serviced some of the 'rest homes' they called them then, that were in the downtown Detroit area. The girls would go after work, a group of them, and they would take punch and cookies and snacks. They would take along entertainment, a music machine to entertain the guests. They always participated in the clothing drive for children. Along with it, they had a Travel Club. I got to do a lot of travel through the Girls Club. Ford has a travel program for all their salaried people, and this was kind of a spin-off from that. They allowed the Ford Girls to use the same package.

The Ford Girls had a representative at each of the Ford plants and officers who encouraged the women in the office to join. Dues were $5, then you were eligible to come to the monthly meetings which were always dinner meetings at Ford Headquarters. We always ate in the dining-room at the meetings. Occasionally they would let us eat in the Executive Room that was up on the top level. They had a garden up there with grass and trees and everything. This was in the Summer and you were all out there in the open on the top of the building. The same chefs that cooked every day cooked an evening meal for the Girls group. The dinner meeting usually numbered about 400 women. After our dinners we would go into the Auditorium in the Headquarters Building which had a beautiful stage. That is where we would have our entertainment. There would always be a little business meeting, at first, it didn't amount to a big deal since the officers had their business meeting at a different time and just brought the results for the general membership.

The Ford Girls usually had the Detroit Symphony at one of their meetings and made a large money contribution to them. You had to pay dues to belong to the Girls Club. Every year the Ford Girls Club sold nuts, pecans and walnuts in pound containers. They sold for $6 a bag with the club making half on the sale. They sold tons of them. I sold over 200 at the schools where I worked. It was a good buy, they were packaged in heavy cellophane and were good quality, choice nut meats. That's where they earned some of the money that they gave to the children's programs that they had. They also were connected with a jewelry company in Greece. There was a store over there that exported china, and they got into this Lladro china. Ford Motor Girls were importing this china from Greece and selling it. They had a booklet with the different selections where you could choose from the figurines. They bought them at a reduced price which was another way they had of making money. They had a connection in Italy where they got pearls, cultured pearls, they weren't the first quality of pearls; probably the second or third. But you wouldn't know the difference. That was a big project that made them a lot of money, selling cultured pearls for Ford Motor Girls Club. They were raising money, again, for community projects. It was called "Ford Motor Girls Club", but its name was changed later to "Ford Motor Women's Club".

We had the Joe Muir restaurants. There was a chain of restaurants, in Detroit and greater Detroit, specializing in seafood. That was our first exposure to seafood. It was the first place I had a lobster dinner. It was a cooked lobster, they brought it in, but it was pretty hard to tackle. You had to break the claws off and pull the meat out of the claws. It is a type of fish that seems to have a lot of bone to it. Not much meat, but it was expensive. Everyone went to Joe Muir's. It was an old place, an old restaurant, but it was clean and well maintained. That was a popular place to go. To celebrate an occasion, or something, you could go to Joe Muir's. Then there was Mario's. It used to be close to downtown but then moved out near the Fisher Building on Second. That was my introduction to Italian food, to eat at Mario's.

Carl's Chop house was another place to eat that I remember. When you went there, they had a glass counter with all the steaks on display. Of all those steaks, just lying there, you would select the steak that you wanted and they would then cook that particular steak for you. They catered to people that way and it was a popular eating place.

There was the Roma Café, one of Detroit's favorite Italian bistros. It was tucked in behind Eastern Market. It's kind of a hole-in-the-wall restaurant, but they catered to the higher class people. They always parked your car. You just pulled up in front and they had men who parked your car for you and got your car for you, because it was kind of a run-down neighborhood there by Eastern Market. We went to the Whitney, out there by the Art Institute. It was the Whitney family home, a prominent lumber baron, David Whitney Jr. is said to have built this big mansion, a polished oak palace, in 1894. It was later restored, converted into a restaurant.

Rouge Park, 1957

By Robert Dombrowski

I grew up in Detroit's West side near Plymouth and Evergreen. I was born in 1950. I lived on a street named Orangelawn and we lived in a brand new home that my parents had built. It was a new neighborhood made up of most World War II veterans returning from the war. It was a beautiful area of brick bungalows built with expansion attics, basements and two bedrooms. Just about everybody had a one car garage in the back yard. My street was between Patton and Brail, three short blocks from Rouge Park.

Rouge Park was a huge park on the West side and it went from Plymouth Road to Warren Avenue, which was about two miles and from Burt Road over to Outer Drive, which was about three miles. The Rouge River ran through the center of it with thick woods along each side for almost a block east and west of either side. The rest of the park was nice lawn that was kept trimmed and cut, along with other facilities like Rouge Pools or Brennan Pools, the official name that was rarely used.

Rouge Pools were three Olympic sized pools, one with a ten meter high diving board. The pools were build around the 1920's and were a phenomenal set of pools that were open all summer, seven days a week. There were AM and PM periods and most of us kids went once, and a lot of us went sometimes twice, a day during the summer. You'd roll your bathing suit up inside your towel and walk inside the front door, boys to the right, girls to the left. Admission was free and you would be given a locker key on an elastic band you wore around your neck. Once you found your locker, you'd put your clothes inside and go take a shower naked.

It was just the way it was back then. After your shower, you would walk by the life guard and spin around. I guess they were looking for sores or something, and then you would put your bathing suit on and go outside to join your friends.

Also in the park was an area called Scout Hollow. It was mostly a wooded area used by the Boy Scouts, but anyone else who wanted to go there could. Another fun area in the park was Derby Hill, which was alongside Warren Avenue. I guess they did run Soap Box Derby races there at one time. In the winter, the park also had a huge ice skating rink with a warming house, wooden toboggan slides and sledding hills. It was all lit up at night and attracted people from all over the area.

Also located near the toboggan hill was the Detroit Mounted Police horse barn. It was kind of neat because the barn was built by the United States Army Calvary and all the police saddles were also provided by the Army Calvary and were from the 1800s. It was fun to watch the police practice riding their horses through the park. The police also had their shooting range inside the park. It was exciting to hear the guns shooting during target practice. When the police were not at the shooting range, the kids in the neighborhood would jump the fence and pick up the lead bullets to use in their Wrist Rocket slingshots.

Another interesting thing at the park was the Army Nike missiles. In a fenced area of about five hundred feet by five hundred feet were about a dozen Nike missiles in underground silos. It was the height of the Cold war and these were surface to air missiles intended to shoot down Russian bombers. Army personnel lived in Quonset huts near the ice rink and about once a week, they would bring the missiles out of the silos to service them. I remember all the kids would gather around to watch.

The park also had a lot of sports leagues like baseball, football and basketball. I belonged to the MicMacs League and we played baseball in the summer and football in the fall. There was also a horse stable in the park where you could rent horses to ride. There were tennis courts and a golf course with a driving range to play golf.

In the spring, you'd fly kites. In the summer there was baseball and sometimes you would find an inner tube and float down the river. In the fall, there was football and then there were all the winter activities. During that time, there was little crime to worry about and the park was a safe place to spend time for young kids like us. At night, I remember the older kids, the teenagers, using the park as a lover's lane. You could see their cars parked all over the park.

I remember the park was very well kept at that time. The grass was well manicured and park attendants would pick up trash using long sticks with nails in the end. The bathrooms were always clean and there were drinking fountains all over the park grounds. It was a wonderful place to grow up and we went there all the time.

Detroit's Film Palaces
By Carol Dolph

In 1959 and 1960, I found great pleasure in attending the Madison Theatre and the United Artist Theatre that were known as movie palaces in the Detroit Theatre District. This area was ranked as one of the largest theatre districts in the United States, dating back to the 1920s.

The Detroit based architect, C. Howard Crane designed the Madison Theater which opened in 1917 and the United Artist Theatre in 1928. The Madison had a Neo-Classic style interior and United Artist had a Spanish-Gothic style interior. Both were elaborate and reminded me of cathedrals which I found breath taking. The Madison had 1,806 seats and the United Artist 2,070 seats, and both theatres were capable of projecting films with 70mm capabilities and had reputations for showing the best in motion pictures on their single screens.

To attend a motion picture in Detroit at either of these locations was a pre-planned event. Tickets were ordered ahead of time so we had reserved seats. Men wore suits, shirts and ties and women in suits or dresses. It was an exciting destination...we were going to a movie palace!

Ben-Hur, starring Charlton Heston came to United Artists in 1959 presented by Metro-Goldwyn-Mayer. They billed this movie as "A Momentous Event in Motion Pictures."

Spartacus had one of the finest casts in the history of cinema events – Kirk Douglas, Laurence Oliver, Jean Simmons, Tony Curtis, Charles Laughton, and Peter Ustinov. In 1960, this motion picture was one of the most expensive made in Hollywood and had an exclusive Michigan engagement at the Madison.

Ushers escorted us to our seats. Usherettes wore Roman-style costumes. We were handed souvenir hard cover books that have become gateways to wonderful memories. We walked on plush carpet, sat in soft padded seats, and ate fresh popcorn. I was in awe!

Both motion pictures were spectacular and relied on casts of thousands, huge sets and scenery. House lights dimmed, overtures played, and the curtains opened. On the screen, there were no previews of coming attractions, no commercials, just an entire evening (or matinee) of family entertainment. The performances were thrilling experiences.

After attending one of these memorable events, we stopped at Metropolitan Wayne County Airport for something to eat. The food was good, the planes were fun to watch, and they were open 24/7, unlike most restaurants.

The Fifties
by Sam Kirkland

Our family spent a lot of time together in the late fifties. We made regular trips together to the show, the theatre and the symphony. Once a month, we would all pile in the car for the drive to Grandma's house. She lived off of McNichols near Livernois.

Dad always slowed down when we drove past Marygrove College. A huge elaborate brick and iron fence totally surrounded the wooded campus. The red brick buildings were mostly obscured from the traffic view on McNichols. We would take turns describing how we would be driving up the winding drive to those buildings when one of us kids were enrolled there for college. None of us ever ended up going there but it was a fun game at the time.

Dad always went up to the door to help Grandma down the wide front steps of her porch. With Dad driving, Mom in the middle and Grandma in the front seat, the four of us kids would share the back seat.

We would often go to the Riviera Theater on Grand River. That was one of our favorite places to go to the show. Although the first run shows were always good, a Grand River outing always meant that we would have dinner at the Pizzeria across the street.

From the sidewalk, large picture windows let you watch two cooks spin the dough, toss it high in the air and catch it over their head, then to whirl it on to a wooden slab paddle. They would load it with toppings before sliding it into the wide ovens.

Because of the size of our family, we always sat at the front round table, closest to the ovens. It is anybody's guess what kind of cheese they used but no other taste or smell could ever compare to those great pizzas.

The Riviera Theater had a circular lobby with glass doors opening to the outside on half of its sides. It had an intricately painted dome. As we waited in the lobby for the next show, you couldn't help but look up at the bright colors. We never quite figured out what style the artwork was but it certainly captured your attention.

We saw a lot of good movies but what stands out in all us kids minds is the trip we could always count on to Truan's afterwards for hot fudge ice cream sundaes.

Grandma made sure that we all got to experience live theatre. I remember her taking us all to the Schubert Theatre when "My Fair Lady" came to town. I bet we could all still sing "Get Me to the Church on Time". The lead singer slipped off the edge of the stage into the orchestra pit during that number but just kept singing as members of the orchestra lifted him back up onto the stage. Funny how something like that stays with you.

Because we had to park so far away, Dad dropped the family off on Jefferson Avenue in front of the Ford Auditorium when we went to hear the Detroit Symphony. We all wanted to run up the long canopied sidewalk but my Mother and Grandmother held our hand and made us walk very properly. The most memorable thing was the sound. It seemed like there were instruments on every side of us. Those early, frequent musical experiences probably were part of the reason two of my brothers took up the clarinet and sax.

Grandma and my Mother didn't go with us when Dad took us to Olympia Stadium to see the Ice Capades. We had to drive up Grand River past the Riviera Theater to get to Olympia. We all recognized the theater. We sat a long way up in the Stadium. It was very cold. Dad told us it would be. But it was worth it. The music was loud. There were a lot of costumes and some great skating. It was a great show.

Memorable experiences, great food and lots of time together as a family. There couldn't be a better way to remember the fifties.

The Fishing Trip
By Stella Greene

It was an unusually warm morning in late May 1957. The wind from the rolled down front seat car windows blew her dark curly hair into her eyes. Emma was perched looking out the back window of the two toned Road Master as it made the right turn off Jefferson Avenue into the riverside city park.

As the powder blue and white Buick proceeded down the park road toward the river's edge, a massive iron stove towered over the car. Probably 40 feet high, the bright sunlight reflected off of the shiny metal trim of the black, white and silver looming structure.

She turned and tugged at her mother's hair. "That cook stove looks just like the one in Grandma's kitchen, except it's much bigger. Do they burn wood in that one too?"

Before anyone could answer, the car reached the boat launch and all eyes were on the toasty brown wooden boat directly in front of them gently bobbing at the water's edge. Earlier in the day, Daddy had towed the boat on the yellow trailer sitting in the adjunct parking lot to the park's boat launch.

Emma could still see the huge cook stove replica in the distance. Her mouth watered as she thought of how good the perch they were going to catch today would taste when Grandma fried them up her special way on her own cook stove. Emma wasn't sure if it was that old wood burning stove or Grandma's incredible knack for making everything she cooked taste so incredible, but the love Grandma put into her cooking shone through.

Racing around to the trunk of the car, Emma filled her arms with the fishing gear given to her. Daddy proudly carried the round, metal red, blue and yellow plaid ice chest and matching coffee thermos Mommy had bought the family for Christmas. The four glass bottles of Vernor's ginger ale inside the ice chest clanged together loudly. Mommy shot Daddy one of those warning glances and he carefully shifted his load so it wouldn't draw her attention. Mommy carried four bright red cushions with dual straps and everyone's hats and jackets.

Emma's big brother Charlie carried the metal tackle box in one hand and the round metal bait bucket in the other. He raced up behind Emma and tried to put the damp, cold bait bucket against her back. She dodged his teasing advance and fell in step beside Daddy as they walked to the waiting boat.

Newly waxed for this inaugural fishing trip of the year, the teak and cherry 16 foot Sea King with its Mercury 20 horsepower outboard engine was the family's pride and joy. Once all the gear was loaded in, everyone took off their shoes and socks. It would take all of their efforts to launch the heavy all wood boat. The late spring water of the St. Clair River was bone chilling cold but no one complained as they heaved the boat free of the slip.

Daddy lifted Emma over the side of the boat and firmly situated her on the center bench before assisting Charlie in and to his assigned spot on the front bench, at the bow. Charlie was Daddy's designed watcher at the front of the boat. Mommy deftly hopped over the opposite side and took her place next to Emma on the center bench.

Charlie took one of the oars and leaning over the side, dug it into the sandy bottom. He held the boat in place while Daddy climbed in at the back of the boat. Mommy assertively grabbed the back of Charlie's pants to assure herself that no one went overboard while Daddy got situated and the motor started. Charlie tried to give Mommy the look but she ignored his stare and held fast to his pants until she chose to let go. He mumbled under his breath but knew better than to let her hear his displeasure.

Daddy smiled briefly as he caught the activity out of the corner of his eye. It was the same every fishing trip, but no one truly seemed to mind.

As the Mercury motor roared, the boat shot forward and cleanly cut through the choppy water with grace and ease. The wind blew against Emma's face and reminded her of the open car windows earlier. But this was so much better. When Emma was on the boat she felt so much freer, so much happier and yet she didn't know quite why. This year she was going to figure out what made these fishing trips so special.

Boats of all sizes and shapes shared the waterway as they trolled to the fishing lanes. Passing fellow boaters waved and nodded to them. A small freighter briefly tooted its fog horn as its wake created additional movement. To the right, the Canadian industrial sector shoreline hovered in the distance. The Michigan shore at this point along the river was dominated by residential and park areas.

Calculating their location by checking the respective shorelines, Daddy cut the motor and motioned to Charlie to lower the anchor. He secured the anchor rope to the brass cleat on the well shined bow and everyone focused on preparing their respective gear for the day's activity. Emma struggled to fasten the flapping chub on her line's hook. Charlie lightly slapped her hand and took the line. Expertly securing the bait, he tossed the line overboard. She watched the shiny chub sink into the water until it disappeared from view.

Daddy lifted the metal lid of the ice chest and withdrew a glass bottle with yellow and green lettering on it. Using the metal bottle opener shaped like a fish, Daddy popped the cap off and held out the coveted bottle to Emma. "Let's celebrate our first fishing trip of the year by sharing a Vernor's", he announced.

As she raised the bottle to her lips and inhaled the carbonation, she coughed slightly. The first sip always seemed to do that. Passing the bottle on to her Mother, Emma made a mental note that everyone seemed to enjoy the Vernor's as much as she did.

Leaning back against one another, Emma and her mother relied on one another for support as they fished. As the day wore on, Emma's senses became keener. She heard the high pitched call of the gulls flying overhead. The cool breeze off of the water intensified the sharp odor coming off of the freshly caught perch. The glare of the sun reflecting off of the water into her eyes made colors appear more vivid. The motion of the waves gently rocked the wooden boat. But most of all, Emma was aware of the sure and certain comfort of her Mother's bony back bracing her up as she drifted off to sleep.

Fifty years later, Emma sits in front of her computer screen, debating where to start. She absently reaches for the can sitting on the side table. She pops the tab on the green and yellow can and raises it to her lips. As she inhales the bubbles and coughs slightly, a faint smile crosses her lips. She is reminded of the feel of her Mother's back against hers. She misses the security of those times.

Emma reverently places the can on the side table. Without hesitation she leans over the key board and on the computer screen------

"It was an unusually warm morning in late May 1957.........."

Small Town Kids
By Richard Smith

Back in the fifties I was a little kid, but as soon as I was able to I began to enjoy hunting. The best pheasant field around here was between Belleville Rd. and Quirk Rd., south of the Expressway. You could get your season limit of birds in one pass through that field. I have never seen anything like it. I used to hunt in the Harmony Lane area, that was the best rabbit field around here. The only house there then was the one that Henry Ford built.

In a small town there were always high school sports for our entertainment; football games, basketball games and the customary "Dime Dances" that followed. The late evening place was the local Drive-In, where we would gather just to talk.

Another thing that I got involved in was coin collecting. My step-father and my mother owned the local theater and I saw a lot of old coins coming through the box office. It was a good source for collecting coins. I would also go down to the bank on Saturday. I got to be friends with a teller who would give me a hundred dollars worth of 50 cent pieces. I would go over and sit in a corner of the bank and take out the coins I wanted, then go back and he would give me another one hundred dollars. He would just hand it to me, I didn't have to sign my name saying, "I owe you $100". He just let me do that; half-dollars, quarters, all the denominations. My uncle, Wylie Pitcher, was also the City

Clerk. I got to go through the Parking Meters money. So, over the years I had a very nice coin collection.

In the Summer time, I used to like to walk along the lake edge, by myself or with my friends. I used to live on a street along the lake and we would spend a good share of the day, just hiking up and down the lake edge. Not too many people ever had a chance to get down there so it was always interesting for kids to get there. Because I worked a lot in the theater my parents owned and an oil company of my father's, there was not a lot of time for play. But, there would be the occasional baseball game on Saturdays, in one of the vacant lots in town. There was always an informal baseball game to be found there.

In the middle of town there was "Victory Park", always a favorite place for kids to gather and play. The biggest thrill was probably the big slide. Of course, we really weren't equipped to go down the big slide unless we had a piece of waxed paper. The waxed paper gave great increase in the velocity you could achieve on the slide. Living close to a lumber yard, we used to sneak into the lumber yard and built forts out of the piles of lumber they had stored in the back. We could get away with it for about a half a day before someone would show up to chase us away.

Another Summertime pastime was going to Susterka Lake. As a pre-teenager, I was even allowed to hitchhike to the lake to go swimming. It was about three miles from home, we would start out walking, but could usually get a lift on the way. We thought nothing about hitchhiking in those days. Susterka Lake was the swimming place. You would always find somebody there that you knew and have a good time.

My understanding was that the lake was a spring that was dammed up. The lake formed was basically a rectangle with a deep 'V' shaped bottom. At the end, where it was dammed up, they had several different levels for diving. I can't remember how high the highest one was, I know it was more than twenty feet above the water. I never got up enough nerve to dive off of that one. Off to one side they had a building where you could change clothes. When you would go to Susterka Lake you had to pay, like 15 or 20 cents and you would get a wire basket for your clothes. The baskets were numbered and they had a safety pin that was numbered. That was your claim-check to get your clothes back. You would just pin it to your bathing suit and it was there when you were ready to leave. They would keep your clothes for you and they sold refreshments there. On both sides of the water they had an area roped off where you could go if you were a non-swimmer. The middle, of course, was the deepest part. In the center there was a raft, floating out there. You could swim out there and climb on. The raft was usually occupied by guys and gals who wanted to be away from the little kids.

The Senior Trip
By Carol (Belaire) Dolph

The Class of '58 at Belleville High School, of which I was a member, had an "once-in-a-lifetime" opportunity to enjoy with our friends, a fun and adventure packed <u>Teen Tour</u> trip to Washington D. C. and New York. This was something that I had never dreamed of. We were told by Teen Tours that more and more classes are making trips. Our brochure was custom printed for the Class of '58 and was worded to add excitement. We would be "experiencing lively activities and thrills as we experienced going from one attraction to another, each of us would be having a good time, and this would probably be the last chance that classmates would do anything as a group."

Let the planning begin! Our six day adventure was going to be $92.75...not including spending money. I just knew it would be worth every penny I earned working at Al's Drive-in as a car-hop at fifty cents an hour. I even worked a double schedule to make sure I had enough money for the upcoming adventure.

We were given our schedule, clothing and what to bring lists, what to pack and a sheet that contained hotel etiquette. On our "What to Pack" list, it was underlined that "t-shirts, and similar type of pull-overs, blue jeans, novelty and souvenir hats, etc., are definitely out of place in hotel lobbies and restaurants." "In public areas of hotels, jackets should be worn". "Girls always wear dresses, blouses or sweaters and skirts....not shorts or slacks". Hotel etiquette suggestions included "do not visit rooms of the opposite sex." "Boys may visit the rooms of other boys; and girls may visit rooms of other girls."

We left Detroit from Michigan Central Station aboard the Baltimore & Ohio Railroad (B & O). While on the round trip train ride, we had our meals in dining cars and our baggage was handled for us. On the train, our curfew instructions included "in each direction....the boys must be out of the girls' end of the car and vice versa, by 11:00 p.m. Daylight Savings Time. At this time, lights will be dimmed in coaches. You must be in your own room at the curfew hour and remain there until 7:00 a.m.

We arrived the second day in Washington D.C. at the Union Station. Our brochure from Teen Tours stated that Washington, D. C. was "The MOST beautiful city in the world....the "Paris" of the western hemisphere....is not only the nation's capitol...but full of gaiety, intrigue, and fun". Talk about excitement, I even took a picture of our Gray Line bus driver Vern! The bus tour included the Bureau of Engraving and Printing, Washington Monument, Smithsonian Institute, Capitol Building, Congressional Library and the Supreme Court. Accommodations were at The Pick-Lee House, air conditioned with a free radio in our room and televisions in the majority of the rooms. The Lotus Supper Club with dinner, dancing and a floor show was our last stop. We were living in style!

Our third day, Gray Line Tours included Arlington National Cemetery-Tomb of the Unknown Soldier, Iwo Jima Memorial-Lee Mansion; Alexandria, Virginia and Mount Vernon; Lincoln and Jefferson Memorials.

Before we left Washington, D. C., Central Photo Company took our class picture. There were 83 students and five chaperons. Central Photo had our class president at both ends of the picture. Oh the marvels of photography.

Early in the evening we boarded the train and headed for more excitement and activities in New York City. Arrival in New York City at the Grand Central Station was pure excitement. Our Teen Tour brochure told us "We were in the largest city in America that drew visitors from every where. It was the political and fun-capital of the world. Glamour thrills and spectacles awaited us." We checked into the famous 2,000 room Taft Hotel with air conditioned rooms, each with a free radio and television set. We had the evening free to explore the surrounding area.

Our tours included boarding the Circle Line Sightseeing Yacht Cruise around Manhattan; Empire State Building, Radio City Music Hall for a film premier and show; tours of United Nations, upper and lower Manhattan. Just before leaving New York City, we had dinner at Village Barn, the Greenwich Village fun spot.

Needless to say, I wanted to stay longer, but our fifth day was over, and it was time to board the train in the evening back to Detroit to arrive early the next morning...our sixth day.

Our senior class trip was as our Teen Tour brochure said it would be. We were carefree, enjoyed wonderful entertainment, had deluxe accommodations, and was pre-planned just for the Class of '58.

One of our class members composed the following on how we saw ourselves:

"For we are the class of '58...
Hurrah! Hurrah!
For we are the class of '58...
Hurrah! Hurrah!
We're the coolest cats in town...
We won't ever let anyone down.
We're the class of '58!
We're rough; we're tough;
We're raring to go! We want
everyone to know.....
We're the CLASS of '58!

It has been fifty years since that trip, and the great memories are still with me.